Jack Hargreaves is amongst the best-known and most popular of television broadcasters. His weekly magazine programme about life in the country, 'Out of Town', was first broadcast in 1959 and ran for twenty-four years until 1981. Its appeal endures, and items from the series continue to be nationally shown.

He was born in the West Riding of Yorkshire into farming stock, moving south as a boy to a farm in the Vale of Aylesbury. In 1929 he went to the Royal Veterinary College. By 1933 he was earning a living writing articles for Fleet Street and scripts for radio. He began working in films, first for Alexander Korda and later for Ealing Studios.

On the outbreak of War he joined the Royal Artillery, later being commissioned into the Royal Tank Corps and serving on Montgomery's staff. After the War, he returned to journalism, and in the early 1950s was editor of both *Lilliput* and *Picture Post*.

Always eager to reach as wide an audience as possible, he was inevitably drawn towards the television, then in its infancy. He joined Southern Television in 1959, both as a programme-maker on 'Out of Town' and as a Programme Controller. He now lives in Dorset.

OUT OF TOWN

A Life Relived on Television

———

JACK HARGREAVES

THE DOVECOTE PRESS

First published in 1987 by The Dovecote Press Ltd
Stanbridge, Wimborne, Dorset BH21 4JD
ISBN 0 946159 46 7

© Jack Hargreaves 1987

Photoset in Palatino by Character Graphics, Taunton
Printed and bound by Biddles Ltd
Guildford and King's Lynn

Contents

The Old Man is a composite of father, grandfathers and uncles; together with old farming friends – in particular Victor Pargeter of Burston Hill Farm.

Introduction – The March of Time

When I was young I heard it said that Queen Victoria had seen the world move forward further in her lifetime than all the monarchs who preceded her.

As a little princess she had her portrait made to send to her great uncle, a Grand Duke somewhere in middle Europe. It was done by a miniature painter on a small piece of ivory and entrusted to an officer who was a Queen's Messenger. He put it in his saddle-bag and galloped right across the continent to deliver it.

Yet before she died she was filmed on the terrace at Osborne.

But she had a slow old time compared to me.

Up to the age of seventeen I went to market every Wednesday at six miles an hour behind a grey pony called Quicksilver. At twenty-three I sailed to America in five days on the *Aquitania* to take part in a programme called The March of Time. At forty-four I had lunch in London, mounted a jumbo jet and, gaining five hours across the Atlantic, attended a meeting on Madison Avenue the same afternoon.

I listened with earphones to Big Ben chiming at midnight on 31st December 1921: it was 2LO, the first station of the British Broadcasting Company. I was still a man in his prime when we watched the astronauts on the moon.

As an army cadet I learned to shoot a single-shot Lee Enfield; and I was blown up in Antwerp by a V2 – the first rocket weapon – in a war which it now dates me to mention.

At twenty-two I was associated with my first broadcast programme, a sound radio entertainment for which there came up from Mr. Cochrane's show at the Palace a pretty girl in an ermine wrap called Jessie Matthews.

At forty-eight I was asked to do a few television programmes about the old agrarian life.

I had little hope for them because I believed people had become uninterested in the past. Anyway, the past crept up closer and closer behind us. In 1986 the BBC, celebrating one of its customary anniversaries, put on a programme which was billed as a 'period gem'. It was made in 1965.

However, to my unending surprise, the 'Out of Town' programmes went on for twenty five years. I received and answered thousands of letters and met many more thousands of people, young, middle-aged and elderly.

I learned that most of them in all generations think that something has gone seriously wrong with the world but can't work out what. And I learned that for many of them the life I lived while I was growing up has become a desirable dream.

This book – like my programmes – is concerned with those times; with the feeling of the old, small-farming life and the know-how of it.

Raven Cottage, Dorset
1987

1
People

It was first revealed to me that people are but a part of nature on a late summer evening long ago when I was following behind the Old Man through Long Wood on the way to set some rabbit snares.

I knew Long Wood very well, every inch of it. It was part of our territory. We walked through it with feet going down flat to the ground and eyes watching without cue from the mind for twigs that might snap underfoot. But something was missing. The noise of the wood pigeons was missing and that meant that Long Wood had been recently disturbed. Not by a fox. The pigeons would not have moved for him. They would have sat still in the elm-trees watching his passage below them with their elderberry eyes.

For us the wood pigeons should have flapped out of the trees, cracking their wings together at each stroke to produce their startling warning. But tonight the pigeons were gone ahead of us. People had passed through Long Wood.

We didn't see much of people, not people who couldn't be accounted for. We knew every family for miles around and could place a good bet on what anybody would be doing at any particular time. We even knew the trot of their ponies and could recognise who was passing by. We met them all on Market Day and heard the news of their lives – the men talking in the Crown and the women in King's Cafe. If the Old Man wanted to emphasise something he would say "I'd stand up in the Market and say it!" It was the centre of the world and our presence there expressed the difference between us and strangers.

There weren't many strangers around during the intervening week. The tramps who endlessly shuffled from one workhouse to the next – pushing old prams and carrying unspeakable bundles – kept mostly to the tarmac road four miles away. If one of them strayed off into the lanes his progress was monitored suspiciously until he was safely back on the turnpike.

Sometimes there were wandering bands of unemployed miners in their uniform of pit-boots, cap and choker. They turned up silently in the yard asking in a few words of a foreign dialect for a job to do in exchange for food. They drank pints of fresh milk and chewed on Mother's fresh bread without a change of expression; then walked off across the depressed Kingdom in search of a better life for their families.

Sometimes we heard a distant roar and dashed across the fields and climbed the bank to watch the motorists go by, goggled and veiled. We waved to the motor-car and cheered it, not knowing that it was on its way to destroy life as our people had always lived it.

That was about it for strangers – except for Bank Holidays. On those several week-ends each year there came the strangest of strangers, the Hikers. They came by train from the towns and set off to stride across the countryside at a pace they could never keep up. Not like the ploughman who cut his first furrow at sunrise walking with his horses at a rate they could maintain unvaryingly till sunset.

The Hikers carried knapsacks and were dressed, both men and women, in very short shorts. Hadn't they ever heard of nettles? Even before we graduated to trousers our knickers came down well over the knee.

So the Old Man and I passed on through Long Wood and, coming round the whiskered bole of an elm-tree, looked down to see below us a true pair of Hikers. They had abandoned their shorts.

I felt my breath stop as I realised they were performing an act with which, as a farmer's boy, I was familiar. Bulls and cows did it. Cocks and hens did it. Hob and jill ferrets did it. Now I saw that people did it. It was not just that we lived in touch with the natural world. We belonged to it.

The Old Man considered the unsuspecting couple in silence. Then he banged the uppermost hiker on the backside with his stick and said, "You'll shut the gate when you go out, young man?"

This was the laconic speech of our elders at its best. They could really distill a situation. Once, during the Kaiser's War, when they were trying to get some emergency organisation into agriculture, a Ministry official asked the Old Man for his private opinion of another man who farmed close by. After a short interval for thought he gave it, "The only bit of ground he's fit to occupy measures six foot by three."

Betty White remains in my memory after sixty years on account of something the Old Man said. She was a nice girl, daughter of a cowman's widow who lived in one of our nearby cottages and she came up to help Mother in order to learn to cook. We were not among those who could think of having servants but sometimes a mother would say "I'll send her up to you. You feed her and teach her to cook". These girls were greatly in demand as wives.

Once again it was on an expedition to Long Wood, this time to watch the badgers, that we sighted Betty White in the bushes with big Harold Brazier, the well-known local ram.

Next morning, as we set off to ride over the moor and count the bullocks, the Old Man banged on Mrs White's front door with his whip and said, "Watch your Betty, Mrs. White, or she'll soon weigh a bit heavier."

He never offered me any comment about the bare-bottomed Hikers. Without doubt he knew how much it had widened my horizons but thought that was probably the best way it could happen. There was nothing we needed to learn about sex. We just had to discover that it also applied to us. Once we had there was no need to refer to the matter again, and they never did. You could be in trouble if your tongue strayed close to the subject in mixed company. Not because that was indelicate but because it was disrespectful.

Old Mr Downfield, famous for breeding shorthorn cows of the Wildeyes strain, lived at the farm below us with his older spinster sister. She was most intimidating in her long-sleeved black dress with lace at the throat and her hair done up tight on top with innumerable pins. Nobody would be disrespectful to Miss Downfield, least of all her brother. When a cow was to be put to the bull in the yard behind the house the matter would not be mentioned to her but, the evening before, her brother would say "Are you going shopping in the morning?" Without looking at him she would reply, "Yes, I shall walk to the ten o'clock bus."

When they'd cleared up in the yard after the morning milking, Mr. Downfield would haul out his pocket-watch to check that it was ten o'clock and Nature could be proceeded with. And the cowman told me that once the proceedings were under way he would look up at the house and be sure to see a curtain moving in the upstairs bedroom window.

My own close acquaintance with Miss Downfield began when I first went to Sunday School. This was unavoidable in our community. After all, the parents had to have some time to themselves. We all worked dawn to dusk, five days a week, went to market on the sixth, and were in chapel on Sunday morning. So, on Sunday afternoons it was the job of the spinster to keep the young confined in the Sunday School. I used to wonder what the bachelor Mr. Downfield did with his afternoon off.

With great strictness Miss Downfield organised our making of sand models of the Valley of Canaan, with little paper palm-trees. She told us stories of the Infant Jesus for whom she seemed to have her one soft spot. And at Christmas she produced quite brilliant children's plays. My own first participation in one of these was to be echoed quite deliciously in later life.

I was only a toddler so I had to be given a toddler's part, one of six robins with beaks on their caps and little red waistcoats, who were to dance a toddling ballet as backing to the star of the show. This was an older girl, dressed as a silver fairy, who was to sing a song composed by the producer and accompanied by her on the harmonium.

The fairy was confident at rehearsal – not to say snooty – but on the night, when the robins had toddled sixteen bars of introduction and she tripped onto the stage, the sight of the audience transfixed her. She froze and, to the accompaniment of the harmonium and the chatter of delighted robins, she suffered a shameful accident.

However, the fairy overcame her stage-fright, went on the stage and became very famous. She quite recently died a Dame with an obituary in *The Times*.

Many years after my performance as a robin I was sitting

in the canteen at Ealing Studios with a party which included the now full-grown fairy, this time dressed as Queen Elizabeth the First. A journalist asked her about her first appearance on the stage and she began to tell him some repertory story. "No", I said. "I was present at your first appearance. I was one of the robins."

For a full minute she dried. Then she said, "God, that there should be any of you wretched little birds alive!"

From Sunday School onwards their Chapel beliefs were strongly held. They had none of the ideas that had come from Wesley but were pre-reformation dissenters – congregationalists. They thought of themselves as descended from the earliest English Christians, from the cells that had held together secretly during the first persecutions. Most of all they were against priests and vestments, shaking their heads over a picture of a Bishop got up in all his gear. Would Jesus have been welcomed in his cathedral? No doubt things had started to go wrong with Saint Paul.

A man's first care must be his own conscience, not those of other people. When you could go to bed every night with nothing to blame yourself for, then you might start on other people. Of course, you could turn a rough tongue on other people as long as you never turned your back on them.

When Mother and the Old Man got married and moved into their own farm at Michaelmas they woke at daybreak to the sound of jingling chains. Out in the yard were the plough-teams from all the four neighbouring farms ready to help them get a start.

From infancy I have known that the effective sanction on a man's behaviour is the opinion of his peers, and that it works best in groups small enough for everyone to know everyone else's business. A branch of the miners' union.

A regiment. A small, specialised factory. Such groups –
sharing a private mystery – naturally act together and have
a resistance to outside influences.

Our sanctions were applied on the chapel steps after
Sunday service. There, before a full audience in their best
clothes, that's when things got said.

"Your lot goes by me home from school, Mary. I hear
your Edith's picked up a word or two she shouldn't know."

"The old black horse will want a bit more grub, Charlie
– if you're going to load the cart up like it was Thursday."

"I reckon Fred'll mend his North End fence soon. If he
don't want his heifers covered by that old screw of Tom
Elliots." A good left-and-right that.

Our private mystery was the land, and life as lived under
the influence of the chapel: but not in either an Anglican
or a Methodist way. I don't think that I ever heard the
word 'sin' outside the chapel walls. They would criticise
us for idleness or greed or for wanting what belonged to
other people. Our consciences were frequently fertilised
but we were never given a sense of sin; and so, I suppose,
we were saved a lot of anxiety.

We knew the local Anglican vicar, Mr Jenkins – a short,
fat, red-faced Welshman with a small stock of laborious
jokes that amused him a great deal. Somehow he had got
himself appointed by whichever of the big-house people
held the living in hand and – particularly after he acquired
a small car – he moved around but didn't try to evangelise
in our area. He never invited us into his house of surplices
but he called pretty often, and always at the same time of
day! Just as we sat down to tea we would hear his booming,
pulpit voice and sight the advancing dog-collar. Like
everyone else he knew the quality of Mother's pasties.

I have often wondered how our ideas would have been

different had we belonged to his flock. As it was, many of the ideas I found current in later years came as a surprise to me.

I was puzzled by the notion of an inequality between men and women. I knew that, in our lives, a man and wife were joint managing-directors; that a great responsibility was shared between them and they faced it in intricate partnership, like two people playing together in a championship match of double tennis.

A farmer who lost his wife was a cripple. A farmer's widow was in trouble unless she had a son well grown up.

I could also not understand why there should be a problem of colour. Up to the time I left the country to go to college I saw only three black faces.

The first used to come to the Market, a little black man who stood behind a table covered with pink bottles. He plunged his hand into a big jar and brought out live snakes to shake at the crowd – I'm sure they were harmless grass snakes. He brandished an elaborately carved piece of wood – I'm sure it was an old table leg. He sold the pink bottles to cure everything, with a strong hint that they could deal with the consequences of misspent youth. I could watch him forever. He seemed to have complete power over the people before him. I never knew his name but the Market Foreman called him The Crocus.

Among the boys I met when I won a school scholarship was one with a dark good-looking face who was brilliant at his lessons. One year on Speech Day his father arrived in long white robes, surrounded by a turbaned body-guard. "My hat", we cried, "have you seen Achmed's pater?"

The other black face I knew very well. It was in our own family album. Huge – with a face polished with Cherry Blossom – he had posed for the photograph in top-hat and frock-coat. His name was Doctor Owidiji-Owijola.

Later I was to meet this negro giant and hear him recite crazy poems for us children, "Halfa Leeaygoo!" he roared, brandishing his walking-stick like a spear, "Halfa Leeaygoo! Unwahd!" It was the opening line of the 'Charge of the Light Brigade'!

More about him later.

2
Places

Our place was built on the pattern of the earliest English small farm houses. A passage cut right through the middle of it between two doors, front and back.

The place was mentioned in Domesday Book but then it would have been just a collection of hovels – probably wattle and daub – that could never have survived the centuries. There might have been a Roman settlement nearby because one corner of the cart stables was built with small flat red bricks that an expert once declared to be Roman. Otherwise there was no trace of it.

Communities of small farmers were created – more probably revived – when the feudal system was hit by the Black Death. The plague killed thirty, perhaps forty per cent of the English people quite suddenly. Originating in the Far East it had reached the Mediterranean at Ankara. In a year it was in Greece. In another in Spain, then it crossed the Pyrenees and arrived in Gascony where the English were fighting the French. It got aboard one of the returning English supply ships and landed at Melcombe Regis in Dorset in the spring of 1348. By Autumn it was in London and then, after raging the country for two years, it petered out.

When it was done the feudal estates were short of people. For the first time working men could argue about where they would work and what for. Wage bargaining – born 1349!

Better than that, on the edges of the hard-hit estates

there was land to be had. The brighter and more independent of the yokels – among whom I count my forefathers – were able to set up on their own.

In most cases they never got possession of the land – through a variety of arrangements like copyholds and cotter's leases – they were able to pass the holdings down through the generations of their families. The feudal barons gave way to Tudor adventurers and there came in turn the East Indian merchants returning with their treasure ships; the capitalists of the Industrial Revolution; finally perhaps – as in our case – the financiers who had accommodated the Prince of Wales during his fifty year wait for the death of the Widow of Windsor.

But through all this time the churchyard continued to sprout with stones that bore the unchanging names of the small-farm families.

Later, when I was in the New Forest, there lived in the cottage opposite us the descendants – still bearing the same name – of the man who found the body of William Rufus and took it to Winchester on his forest cart.

On their new holdings they built themselves small rectangular houses – using local materials and thatching with straw or reed or heather. They built them with a passage through the middle between two doors front and back.

In the space on one side they lived – calling it the house-place. They kept their stock safe from the weather in the other space and the name of that was the byre. The house-place was planked over at wall height to make a sleeping-loft under the eaves. It was the scene of many of the goings-on recorded by Chaucer. When I was little we still knew one family that climbed up to bed with a ladder.

The byre was also boarded over to make a loft where

the sheaves of corn could be put safely in the dry at harvest-
time. Later on the front and back doors were opened so
the wind could blow through to carry away the chaff and
they threw the sheaves down into the passage to be
threshed with the flails. Thus this entrance passage came
to be called the threshold. I suppose we should not properly
talk about a bride being carried 'over the threshold' but
'through the threshold'.

Grandfather's house still had a bedroom that extended
over a cow-byre and when I slept in it my lullaby was the
sound of munching and the clink of chains.

Over the centuries the houses were refurbished and developed. Glass became cheap enough for such windows
as ours, but the original shutters were left in place. Dormer
windows cut into the thatch brought light to the upper
floor. Flagstones covered the earlier floors of stamped earth
mixed with lime and cowdung. And then came the stair-
case, narrowing the threshold for half its length.

The last of the changes came around 1840 with the railways. Midland brick for an extension to the dairy. Welsh
slate to replace the thatch. The landlords bought these
materials by the waggon-load and they were brought to
the nearest siding to be fetched as needed by the builders'
carts. You can stand in the middle of almost any English
village now and recognise the difference between the pre
– and post-railway houses.

As a fifty-five year old – when the old folks had gone
and War and work had kept me moving around the world
– I went back to take another look at the house. It was not
there. It had been compulsorily purchased as part of the
scheme to build a new reservoir which was then cancelled
through a cutback in public spending.

It had stood there from Domesday to the time of the

Welfare State. Then it died of bureaucratic indecision.

The ruined buildings stood among furze and heather that had crept down from the hill and a gamekeeper came to ask me what I thought I was doing. Against a wall that had collapsed to three feet high Mother's kitchen range stood rusting.

Our young days began at the kitchen stove. In those days it was blacked, with bright edges.

Somebody – and it was usually a boy – came down first to get the cows in for the morning milking. You brushed out the grate then went to the barrel in the scullery for a big double handful of nicky-wood. This was the twigs broken from the ends and sides of faggots and when you crushed the grate tight full with a few bigger pieces on top it would blaze up without the aid of paper at the first touch of the match. It would boil the big black kettle and still start the coal that you put on afterwards.

Having dealt with the tea-pot you fetched two tight faggots from the woodshed, kicked one of them into the funnel under the copper and stood the other alongside. Then you shouted to the others that tea was ready and made for the great outdoors.

Mother came down when everyone else had started in the cowyard. She had the place to herself till breakfast-time. It was still three hours before school.

The domestic arrangements seemed to me satisfactory and not involving any more work than was to be expected. The wood shed was set alongside a flagged path that led to the outside privy. Everyone had to pass it and knew not to come back empty-handed. When the open hearth with its spits gave way to the iron kitchen-range a coal-shed was added along the same route, so you went out with an empty coal-bucket and came back with a full one.

The copper gave us constant hot water just for the trouble of kicking the faggots. As the first faggot burned away you gave it a little inward kick at every time of passing; then when there was room you moved the next one into place and thenceforward kicked that. It was like a little dance to be executed when crossing the scullery.

A long-handled pump stood alongside the sink with a pipe down to the well and a dipper on the draining-board. Every time you dipped out hot water you returned the same number of dippersful of cold from the pump. So, what with kicking and dipping, you knew there was always about twenty gallons of hot water on hand.

Life was lived in the big kitchen with the giant scrubbed table that wore a chequered oil-cloth at mealtimes. On a dresser that covered the whole of one wall was arranged the crockery, all blue Willow Pattern and other related designs. People liked that best. They called it 'Delph'.

We got our light from paraffin lamps of which there would be three in the kitchen at night when homework, sewing and newspaper reading were all being done at once. The smell of well-kept oil lamps was delicious. It's still the smell of home.

At supper-time a row of candles was put on the cupboard in the passage, each with its box of matches, and when you went to bed you took one to light your own way up. Later on Mother would turn up to take your candle away and stop you reading in bed.

We made contributions to modernisation in our generation. Once the Old Man decided that Mother deserved the dignity of an electric front-door bell in place of the old iron knocker. On a shelf high up in the passage were placed two big square glass jars full of an acid mixture with metal rods sticking down into them. It was a battery, he ex-

plained. For a week Mother's cooking was disorganised
by her having to go out every five minutes to press the
bell then nip back to see if she could catch it still ringing.
All the neighbouring wives came over for a press. Thereafter it was never used. After all the door was never shut.
Everyone – from the landlord to higgler – just walked right
in and shouted Hello.

Our biggest decision was to install running water. On
the hill, well above the house, there was a continuous
spring. The water that soaked into the heathland cap on
Lines' Hill at this point met more impervious soil and broke
out through the surface. Here we made our reservoir. It
was about the size of a big shed and was lined with bricks.
It had a top of railway sleepers and a post with a pulley-
block so it could be raised by a chain, a nail being put
through one of the links to hold it safe. We raised it now
and again. There was never any trouble but we liked to
look at the frog. The frog had somehow got in there at the
beginning and had lived there ever since. He looked very
well though he was pure white from living in the dark.
He kept it all quite clear of insects. We called him Chalky.

The plumbing and piping we did for ourselves. There
is an old saying that a boy brought up on a farm can do
absolutely anything – rather badly! It has some justice since
the jobs are mostly done in a hurry and most of the materials
are scrounged. Our piping was gathered chiefly from abandoned wartime establishments around the country. It was
very heavy and in several different sizes. In the end we
got it together and it worked very well: but you certainly
noticed it.

So we got a bathroom and said goodbye to tin baths on
the flagstone floor. So we got a boiler behind the range
and no longer had to kick the faggots. So we got a W.C.

and the earth privy stood unused.

This latter in my opinion was a mistake. The earth privy has no equal as a means of human waste disposal. It looks after its own job and its residue goes nowhere except into the chemistry of your own soil. If it's dug more than fourteen feet deep its decomposition will keep pace and it will never fill up.

Of course, you couldn't have them in cities, hence the horror and expense of modern sewage disposal. In later times I made a documentary on this subject and learned that the waters of the Thames pass sixteen times through the human gut on the way from Oxford to London. I learned also that the cities of the world empty into the ocean every year a mountain of excrement as high as Everest and sixteen miles on the square of the base.

But you could still have them in the countryside. My young brother became Medical Officer of Health in a coastal district and several times met the crisis of typhoid caught in London restaurants through oysters from his local beds. Each time he took water samples over miles until he located the dwelling of the unconscious carrier. Each time he cut off the plumbing and transferred the carrier to an earth privy. So the oysters became safe again.

I think that out of town we should be allowed to maintain our natural advantage.

Our next step into the twentieth century was the electricity. The Farmers Union did a deal. If we put the posts up across our land the Company would wire us up. So we spent a whole winter putting up posts, across Joe Payne's land and then Charlie Elliott's and then ours. This brought an unexpected bonus. At places where we had to leave the hedge-line and cross a field there grew at the bottom of each post, where the hay-mower couldn't cut, a patch of tall, rough grass. Perfect nesting places. In two years we had twice as many partridges. From then on each tuft was protected with a circle of sheep netting.

When we finally got switched on we had a little Belling stove in place of the Primus on which Mother had made the breakfast every morning while the range got hotted up.

But her greatest joy was to be rid of the oil lamps. Every day without fail she had brought them down to the scullery to be perfectly cleaned and trimmed. It was the only way to keep the smell down. Now she emptied the lot and stuffed them up in the attic. When life finally ended for us at the farm they were just left behind.

There were six of them and four were made entirely of deep blue Bristol glass. I suppose that in the end some travelling knocker bought them and sold them to an antique dealer who put them in one of the containers he was sending to America. I think of them now – odourless and in their turn electrified – decorating the side-tables of some Dallas mansion.

Having the posts we quite soon got the telephone; the old pillar phone where your voice made patterns in a canister of loose carbon granules. The Old Man never got the idea. He didn't grasp that it worked by electricity. He thought it was some kind of tube through which, if you made enough effort, you could transfer your voice to the Market Town or even to London. "Can you hear me?" he roared, "Don't hang up! Can you hear me?" We could hear him across the yard above the noise of the barn engine.

In later years, just before he died, I rang him up from a far country. He was still doing it. In fact, realising that this was the furthest his voice had ever had to travel he outdid himself.

So – in our turn, in our generation – we brought the old

house into what was perhaps its sixth century though every day it reminded us of its past and of ours.

Once, when we decided to do up the parlour, the removal of three layers of Victorian wallpaper revealed that the lime and cowhair plaster below was crumbling and as it was removed we saw that the walls beneath were covered with perfect black oak linenfold panelling. It had to belong at least to the fifteenth century.

Unfortunately the builder told the agent and he told the landlord. Orders came for it to be removed, peg by peg, to a new small room built onto the Hall to receive it. We lost the use of the parlour for three months.

I suppose they had some kind of title to it. Undoubtedly it belonged first in the old Abbey on the edge of whose land we had probably managed to settle after the plague. Then, at the time of the Dissolution, the Abbey was ruined and pillaged and no doubt our antecedents carried the panelling down in triumph. At the same time the land was given to the first of the many landlords preceding ours.

We didn't point out to them the shallow quarter-circular carved stone sink that was Mother's bird-bath in the garden.

From the time I began to learn about such things I have been convinced that it was a Holy Water stoop.

3
Mother's Day

Mother used to say that the worst day of her whole life was that of her betrothal.

She was one of the Jubbs who had a farm some way over. Her name was Ada. Her mother was Hannah, her sister was Sarah and her two brothers Joseph and David – all Bible names. They used to prick for them. When a boy-child was born they pricked a pin into the closed bible leaves then opened it at that page and read on. The boy was given the first man's name they came to – except Jesus or Judas. We had them all in the district – Lukes and Noahs and Ezekiels. It was the same for girls but I don't know if there were any excluded women's names. I don't remember a Delilah.

When she was eighty-two she could still walk six miles a day. She started doing it at the age of six on her way over the hills to school. Three miles in the morning carrying two cans of milk that had to be delivered to cottages on the way and three miles back at teatime, stopping to pick up the empty cans.

If there was any light left after tea her father sent her out in the field to pick up stones in a bucket. If it was dark she sat on a three-legged stool alongside Great Aunt Emma's chair and practised her sewing. The old lady seemed not to take much notice, but then she'd suddenly look down and say, "Pick out those last three stitches and do them again even."

She was still a teenager when the Old Man started to

walk her home from Chapel, and they made up their minds before the families did. Her people didn't want her to go off too soon because she was useful at home; and Grandfather thought that if his eldest son got married he would soon be pressing on his heels to take over the farm. If that happened then the grandparents would have to 'go to the cottage'. It was the strict custom but it felt like the end of life to an older farmer.

But soon there was news of the trouble in South Africa and talk that the Volunteers might be called upon. If that happened then the lad would be going off with the Yeomanry. So everyone decided that the thing might be allowed to go as far as betrothal and it was the last custom concerned with this that gave Mother her bad day.

One Sunday morning the Jubbs came over early. They arrived behind their black cob Jessie with all the family packed in the float, together with several big laundry baskets covered with white cloths and packed with provisions. Mother was holding her apron wrapped up in brown paper. Grandmother had got the Hargreaves' kitchen clean and tidy with the range burning nicely and it was into here – after a little polite conversation – that the eighteen-year-old Ada Jubb was led and her baskets carried in after her. Then both families went off to Chapel leaving her on her own.

She told me that she was terrified as she put her hand into the ovens to try and get the feel of them. She found the flat irons and put one on each of the cooking rings. After ten minutes – which she spent examining the strange pots and pans – she took off the irons and spat on each of them to see how much heat there was at each point on the stove-top. Then she took a deep breath and started to cook Sunday dinner for fourteen. By the time the ponies rattled back into the yard she had the table laid and the house was filled with the smell of food. She'd given it her best shot, as the Americans say. She'd added a few specials. By each place there were blobs of her own made cream-cheese on little rush-mats she'd plaited. Big onions, hollowed out and stuffed with kidneys and bacon – an invention of hers that I was to enjoy many times later. Perhaps it was those onions that gained me the chance to be born.

The meal was eaten almost in silence, with Mother not daring to look at anyone, but afterwards Grandfather said with an air of decision 'You've done great, lass'. They were engaged.

That Sunday dinner was eaten in 1897. Nowadays it would be seen as a very sexist ceremony. In fact it was a job interview which she was always going to pass, and not for a junior job. It was the interview for a full partner-ship.

After that they walked from Chapel arm-in-arm, but only for a week or two because the call for the Yeomanry came.

It was a call for both men and horses. The Yeomanry in those days all mounted themselves. The men from the big houses turned up on their hunters, turned overnight into officers, and from the farms the rank and file rode in on their cobs. The district was famous for black horses of the cob stamp, all descended from the pack-horses that used to bring the lead ore down from the hills.

Grandfather was scratching his head over which of our two the lad should take when old Mr Crowther drove into the yard with four of his best tied on behind. He was one of the top breeders but he'd never had any sons. He was determined that his stud was going to serve, so the Old Man went off on Mr Crowther's Ebony.

They'd given themselves time to make the march slowly

and harden the horses. One hour's trotting, half-an-hour's walking, half-an-hour's leading and then fall out for ten minutes; so in the small hours they came to Liverpoool where the whole place was dark except for a few flares at the dock when they went aboard. In that way it came about that the first city ever to be seen by the country lad who became our Old Man was Cape Town.

They went as lads to South Africa and came back as hard men. They understood nothing of the causes of the war and knew not who the Boers might be. The Queen had called them so they went. It was a surprise to find they were fighting small farmers like themselves.

The war had something of the flavour of the famous Duke of York, except that it was Lord Methuen who marched them up and down again. The Generals, who had risen from the best regiments, formed the men up in lines and squares and advanced them in blocks. The Boers who could hit a sandy-coloured line at half-a-mile with their Mauser hunting rifles, sat with their ponies tied behind the nearest rock and took pot shots. On the British flanks waited groups of Lancers, their pennants fluttering, looking with field-glasses for someone to charge.

Some British troops had been sent out at first wearing red coats, but now they changed them all to a new camouflage kind of colour. In celebration of this a little china figure was put on sale all over Britain and Mother bought one. I still have it. It is called 'A gentleman in Kharki' and, although they explained politely that the word was derived from the Hindustani for 'Dusty', any soldiers – or any Londoner – can tell you what the 'Kakker' is.

After four ignominious defeats in a month they sacked the generals. They were not disgraced, of course, but went back to their clubs and fulminated over the outrage of the command having been given to some little Gunner from the Bengal Army whose second-in-command was, unbelievably, a Sapper.

However, Lord Roberts and Kitchener did the job well, and the yeomanry did well too. They operated like the Boers as mounted infantry – riding across country and dismounting for the fire-fight – they and the Australian Light Horse with whom they made friends and whose big felt hats they adopted.

Once the Old Man distinguished himself. They were sitting on a kopje with orders to hold it when the troop officer was shot through the head by a Boer sniper. The lad, now a Sergeant, found himself in charge. They hung on for ten days until some Highlanders got up to them, and didn't touch their iron rations until the fifth day.

He was decorated for that; and then he was court-martialled for allowing the men to eat their iron rations without the order of a commissioned officer. It was a formality, the kind of thing the army has to do when there are written regulations, and the members of the court shook hands with him afterwards. But he never forgave them for putting him on trial. "What was I supposed to do when they were hungry?" he said, 'Dig the bugger up?"

He lasted till Paardeberg where things first turned for the British and there he watched the first Boer General drive in to surrender. Tall, sharp eyed De Wet, bearded like a prophet. Most of all he remembered the Boer's cross-country cart on two five-foot wheels. It was pulled by a pair of Basuto ponies, one each side of a pole and rode across the veldt like a good boat in a sea. The Old Man memorised every strap of the tack for doing it.

Then he went down. Thanks to Lord Bobs' disinterest in medical services, typhoid diseases killed three times as

many British soldiers as the Boers did. He came home in
a hospital ship full of enteric victims.

He had seen the breadth and beauty of South Africa
where, in the crystal air, a two-day march looked as if it
could be done by dinner-time. He had seen each in turn
of the hundred men lying in a marquee with him crawl to
the ditch down the middle and squitter his guts out. At
intervals he had seen three British soldiers who had
marched too long into the fire of an invisible enemy shot
for cowardice. He had seen drunken Regulars testing a
struggling Boer woman for VD with the use of a polished
brass cartridge case. He had seen lions and hyenas.

And another thing. When the yeomanry went to Africa
nearly a hundred years ago they were astounded at the
situation of the blacks. The whites had turned their backs
on them. The chapel men couldn't keep it off their own
consciences. A while later they found a young black boy
who had been taught English at a missionary school. Pool-
ing their pay, and writing home to their chapels for funds
to be raised, they brought him to England and sent him to
medical school. I'm told that when he went back he was
the first qualified black doctor ever to practice in Africa.
His name was Owidiji-Owijola.

The Old Man came back thin and tired and went to
Mother for comfort. As soon as she saw him coming she
put the kettle on.

He had brought her a treasure. Even he knew something
about current fashions and their wedding was on the way,
so he had been to an ostrich farm and spent a lot of money
on two perfect white plumes and watched them packed
carefully in a thick hollow bamboo with the ends sealed
with sealing-wax.

When they opened it – it was empty. Someone had broken

it open to steal them and then sealed the end up again. When you looked carefully you could see where he'd done it. The Old Man was sure without question it would be one of the hospital orderlies and Mother was frightened there'd be a murder if he met a man in the market-place wearing a badge that said R.A.M.C. He used to say that it stood for Rob All My Comrades.

The returning soldier was well looked on. This was the time of the Khaki Election. Some of the local men had not returned. When they married they got what in other times might have been waited in vain for – a farm of their own.

When they drove over to meet the agent and walk the place the Old Man took a spade with him. Without a glance at the house he was out in the fields digging holes here, there and everywhere. He snuffed at handfuls of earth and dived into ditches to see which way the water flowed. When he was done he came back and said to her "House alright?" "It'll do" she said. And that's the place where all three of us brothers toddled our first steps.

From then on for fifty years they took every big decision together. He used to sum up matters slowly and solemnly and then say "What do you think to it, Ada?"

However, beyond that they divided the responsibility and the financial control between them as it had always been done between the men and women.

All the dairy products – apart from milk sold liquid – all the poultry and the fruit and kitchen-garden were hers. These things could be dealt with round the homestead and wth all of them the youngest children could be useful and so learn how to work. Kind words and kisses were earned by shelling peas and cutting up rhubarb for jam.

The cream was risen in yard-long lead pans along the wall of the dairy and skimmed with a perforated ladle. We bought a separator later but, for all the years the cream went in the 'leads' I've never suffered lead poisoning. The butter was turned in a barrel-churn and each pound marked with two Tudor roses. The buttermilk went into scones and onto oatmeal at summer breakfast. Sour milk became her famous cream-cheese, hanging in bags of cheese cloth and dripping into the leads. For hard cheese we went to old Mr Crowther who specialised in it. We would walk along his cheese-loft as he plunged his little plug-cutter into one seven-pound truckle after another. He kept sniffing and saying "We'll have to find you a right smeller."

She pickled eggs in buckets for the winter, sorted out her hatching eggs and packed fresh eggs in baskets for the market. She was enttitled to an allowance of corn from the barn for the poultry work and would haggle with the Old Man to get it increased as her production rose. She was a wonderful plucker of birds, keeping the feather she wanted and sterilising them for cushions and pillows, but she expected to have birds killed for her. She would put a bunch of cockerels in the shed and say she wanted them by afternoon. As a child I could break a chicken's neck so neatly and quickly that you wouldn't know when it happened. Geese were different. I was stumped the first time she told me to bring her a goose in. The Old Man had to teach me the trick which involed standing on a walking-stick. Nowadays of course – with the revival of Xmas geese – they are killed with a .22 air pistol held against the head like a humane killer. Very neat and efficient.

Her turkeys had the gleaning of our stubbles. She was a fine hand with turkeys which in those days was a skill to be wondered at because there was as yet no inoculation against blackhead and most people lost the majority of the birds they hatched. Hers never seemed to get it. Any morning after the corn was cut you'd see them rush out of the shed when she opened up and go flapping and squawking down to the cornfields like a flock of vultures.

She filled the cupboards with jam and bottled fruit and jars of salted beans. With bacon in the chimney and clamps of potatoes and carrots and parsnips we got through the winter in the days before freezers.

Every morning she made a formal inspection of the kitchen garden and ordered what she wanted indoors. Once it was cut or gathered it was hers, but we had to grow it. We took great pride in the crops for which we'd been responsible when we saw them on the table or being packed for market. To this day kitchen-gardening is one of my greatest pleasures and I hardly know the name of a garden flower. There was no time or space for flower gardening, though Mother had her favourites along the front of the house and roses over the doors. Still, who needs it with fields full of buttercups and hedges of sloe blossom, foxgloves and campions in Long Wood.

Nobody ever knew how much money Mother made – or any other farm wife – it all went into a secret store. Every farm girl knew that when she was to be married it would be her mother who came up with the trousseau. Some of them in time of trouble have been known to produce enough money – some of it handed down from a grand-mother – to save the holding. At their Silver Wedding Mother went out and bought the Old Man a trotting cob he'd had his eye on but thought he couldn't afford. He was speechless.

With it all she cooked for seven hungry people, every meal except Wednesday mid-day. She baked every day in the range and fired the old brick oven on Mondays to make bread that lasted fresh for the week. The rest of Monday she spent in the wash-house. She must have had fifty yards of clothes – line up on the drying ground.

Her steak and kidney puddings cooked on the back of the stove for two days until the flavour came right through the inch of suet crust. Every day at teatime her pasties came out hot – tarts of short pastry piped round the edges and filled with jam or sultanas, apple slices, lemon curd, treacle and breadcrumbs or young rhubarb. When things were bad she fed us, even if she might say "If you want any more it will have to be bread and gravy." In the first World War she picked up a tip from a refugee Belgian lady – lumps of stale bread, soaked in milk, covered with jam and cooked in the oven. She called it 'Pain Purdoo'.

I remember her with wonderment. Every day she was out of her pinny and into a proper dress at teatime to spend the rest of the evening knitting and sewing. She made everything we wore until we went away to school on scholarships. Then she fished out the money for our grey flannel suits.

I never heard her raise her voice in anger nor show a trace of panic. Once as a child on a bicycle I was knocked over by a motor-car on its way to the agricultural show – a Rolls Royce I'm proud to say. Mother opened the back door and found the neighbour standing there with me over his shoulder like a sack. "Ada" said the next door woman "How dreadful. Didn't you faint?" "That wouldn't have done much good," she said.

4
Market Day

The way we used to live in the days before the motor car is still quite clearly shown in the motoring maps of today. Apart from the motorways and trunk-roads that have come later, the land can be seen to be dotted with small country towns fed by converging roads in a spiders-web pattern.

They were born as the countryside opened up, each one in turn being granted its royal charter to hold a market, and each one set in an appropriate place – a ford, a church site, a junction of old tracks – and each one becoming the centre of an intact community. If you stand back from the map the whole thing looks as if it had been done by a wallpaper designer.

Wherever you lived one of these market towns was within seven or eight miles. Just over an hour behind a smart trotting pony. Two hours pull for a heavy horse load. Two and a half hours trudge for a cottage woman with a market basket. The town was the life-centre for all the folk who lived within the same range in all directions. That community had a distinctive life, a recognisable style of harness, thanks to the town saddler; a certain cut to a riding-coat, made by the same man who made your father's; certain words and phrases derived from happenings known to everyone. In our area we built square hay-ricks while those surrounding us built them round.

For six days a week the market towns slept but on market day it was standing room only. There were thirteen pubs in our small town and they all made their living by being open from ten to ten on Wednesdays.

The forward screen of this weekly invasion was made up of the drovers, each coming down one of the spider-leg roads and having started before the sun rose. Nothing like the drovers is to be seen today, except perhaps the poor old ruins who sleep out in London. One of them wore a sacking skirt and farm boots, sucked a clay pipe and was known as the Morphadite. Like the others, he, or she, appeared on Market day then disappeared across the land in the evening to materialise next dawn at the head of some distant road and trudge down to another market. They were mighty drinkers. Their voices were hoarse with shouting and sleeping in damp ditches, and they quarrelled like bad-tempered dogs. By mid-day on Wednesday the Morphadite could be seen locked in a ferocious stick-battle outside the Crown Tap.

On our road the drover had a shaven head of red bristles and was a walking lexicon of obscenity. In honour of his fighting days – which must have been back in the Crimea – he was known as Old Glory. The system depended on him, since there were no stock-trucks in those days, and I used to meet him at daybreak once every several Wednesdays.

We would have milked before sun-up since there would be a cow or perhaps a few lambs that had to be driven two miles down to the turnpike in time to meet him. Waiting there in the mist we would hear the shuffle of his approaching drove, the mutter of his oaths and the yelping of his two old blue cattle-dogs. They would all come along together, moving quietly like a family. It was amazing how he controlled them. A few pigs under a net in the front of the float. Behind them, with its legs tied on a pile of straw, a calf whose mother followed close, touching it with her nose and blurting softly. Sometimes a farm-horse for sale haltered alongside her, and more than likely Glory would have loaded him packwise with two crates of somebody's geese. He pushed the rest of the mixed drove on in front, nipping in the gateways and whistling to his dogs, while the float-pony followed behind. As they moved on against the red sunrise we turned home for breakfast.

After breakfast on market day we put on our best leggings. Mine were of soft-brown buckskin, a present from an uncle so I could ride one of his ponies at the local show. They needed a lot of work with the button-hook.

Leggings were the farmers' trade-mark – like the parson's dog-collar – until after the Kaiser's war. Then came millions of pairs of gumboots, the surplus of four years trench warfare. Gumboots and barbed-wire were the War's legacy to the countryside, together with the khaki great-coats that the shepherds and ploughmen wore in winter-time. But we still put on leggings for market day.

I put the brush over Quicksilver and got her into her good tack, then took down the bow-topped whip that hung over a bobbin fastened with a twisted pipe-cleaner. Mother's baskets were loaded into the dog-cart and we were off to town – a journey that was punctuated with much waving of the whip and tipping of caps.

The Old Man exploited fully the advantage of a horse-vehicle which was high enough for looking over the hedges, even standing up to get a better view; and while you did so the pony could be relied upon to stay on the road. As we drove along he issued his weekly critique of the farming that went on around us. One man's lambs could have grown better; another's hedge-laying wasn't going to win any prizes; yet another's hay-rick had settled one way on account of faulty building. I always thought he had an unfair advantage through our place being at the end of the line. Nobody had to pass us but we passed everybody.

By the time we got to market, Glory had penned our animals and got the numbers. He stood there, cap in hand, wearing an old soldier's look of dishonest respect, while we paid him his rate for each animal.

Then we all parted. Glory shuffled off to the Crown Tap. The Old Man went up to the cattle end of the market, bound later for the Farmers Ordinary. Mother went down to the small-stock and dairy end, to move on after selling-time with all the other ladies to the King's Cafe where the domestic news of the district was exchanged. We joined all the other boys to roam the whole area in search of possible excitement.

Most of that gang of boys is dead now and the rest of us are old men. All those remaining will remember when the Jersey bull went wild and closed the market for an hour, tearing around with four men on the bull-stick and flinging them all against the wall with just the strength of the muscle between his nostrils; and the day when two wild heifers ran into the hairdressers and drove a pack of ladies all draped with white napkins out onto the cobbles. We watched the drovers fighting. We sat on the railings and listened to the bold tales of Phil Oliver the colt-breaker in his cord breeches, baggy cap on a mop of hair and a ragged stick banged against his high boots for emphasis. We never knew we would one day watch his son show-jumping for England on the television.

The day came when each of us in turn graduated to the Farmers' Ordinary. It was the coming-of-age.

In the bar of the Crown the farmers gathered, most of them with a fad for drinking whisky and milk. Twenty different conversations on weather and prices proceeded. Quietly you found yourself a place in the corner – but there was no hiding-place.

Old Mr Payne emptied his glass and put it down. The bar fell silent. Forty pairs of wrinkle-buried eyes were on you.

"Well now. It's the boy from Burston. Grown up, have you?"

"Yes, Mr Payne."

"What bin doing then?"

"Working, Mr Payne."

"Something more beside, I expect?"

"I've been making a couple of ponies."

"Shooting too? I think I heard you?"

"Yes, Mr Payne."

"What kind of gun you got?"

"Twenty-bore, Mr Payne, single barrel."

"Oh ah. Not many of them about. Can you get the cartridges?"

"Yes, in the square."

"You must be the only one buys them, I dare say?"

"Might be, Mr Payne."

From his pocket came a small yellow empty cartridge-case. God, I thought, he's saved that up six weeks.

"Then what's this bugger doing in my Ram Close?"

"Ah yes, Mr Payne. I remember that. I shot and wounded a pigeon over our Great Ground. Saw it come down over your way. Didn't want to leave it wounded. It wasn't till I picked it up I opened the gun."

Quiet smiles all round. "Well done, lad" said Mr Payne. "Have a drink." Phew! First stage of initiation over.

The Farmers' Ordinary was held in the big dining-room of the Crown. An Ordinary is a meal with a fixed menu. That was the English name for it until they imported the foreign phrase of 'Table D'Hote'. In the days of road travel there were Coaching Ordinaries. At week-ends at the pub on the green there was a Cricketing Ordinary. The Farmers' Ordinary at the Crown was eaten every Wednesday for over a hundred and fifty years.

The tables were set in a big letter E. Along the three arms the families had their inherited places, but to the back of the E – the top table – the farmers graduated by seniority. Joe Payne sat in a high chair in the most honoured place of all. We were halfway down the bottom side next to the Dickens, with the Jubbs opposite.

I think that the fixed menu of those days is unlikely ever to be served again.

The joints of meat on big Crown Derby dishes were carried in by the girls and set in front of the top-table farmers, each of whom was already putting his carving knife to the steel. There was roast beef and lamb and boiled mutton, salt beef and veal. Every joint had been raised and finished by a man in the room. It was like a wine-tasting except that nobody tasted a little. In fact, giving an ear to the general opinions, you might start with a plate of roast beef and then pass up to another carver for boiled mutton.

Bowls of fresh vegetables kept coming to the table. There were jugs of draught beer from Tommy Gurney's brewery at Rowsham. 'Rowsham Brook' they called it. It would gladden the hearts of the real ale boys nowadays.

On my first visit I sat next to Charlie Dickens. He kept an eye on me and talked about horses. What else? He was a Yeomanryman of the generation following the Old Man. His war was the Kaiser's War when they loaded their own horses to join Allenby in Mesopotamia. I'm told it was the last time British yeomanry went to war on their own horses. Of course, after a while of chasing the Turks they had to be remounted. That's when Dickens got his job of sergeant-roughrider.

The remounts came unbroken from New South Wales, to be landed at Tel Aviv. Behind the port they built a half-mile racetrack with six-foot plank fences. Each of the 'Walers' was saddled in a crush and then came bolting out rodeo-fashion with a roughrider on his back. They galloped them round and round the blind track to a standstill. After a couple of goes of that they were sent up and issued to the troopers. They reckoned that by then they'd be alright for a man brought up with horses.

"God, what a job." I said.

"Best job I ever had" said Charlie Dickens. "We only had to do five a day. I used to do mine before breakfast and have the day off." We spent our young lives wondering if we could live up to them. I sometimes look at Harvey Smith and see him as a yeomanryman.

At the end of the Ordinary they brought in china bowls of pipe tobacco and set them along the tables. Then I saw churchwarden pipes smoked as a matter of course. The long pipes were in a rack on the wall, varying in colour from chestnut brown to white. It was not creditable to break the family pipe and have to buy a new one.

The Ordinary had been eaten weekly through good times and bad times. It was the difference between being a farmer, however small, and trying to raise a family in a cottage and garden. Once a week, at least, they ate the best of what they produced. None of them would have thought he could kill a bullock for home, or even a lamb, especially not when milk could only be sold at a loss or the price of wool fell from a shilling a pound to three-halfpence in a fortnight.

I used to think in later years that the landlord must often

have waited for his money. The farmers paid when they sold, settling the big bills when they took a load to the corn-merchant or sent a bunch of bullocks to the Christmas market. They were often very slow but fiercely proud that they could be trusted. I remember when the feed-merchant changed hands, bought out by somebody bigger from further away. On Wednesday the Old Man picked up some stuff and on Friday morning there was an unexpected letter. It contained an invoice. Red in the face he shouted at me to put the pony in and, for the first time ever known, drove into town on a Friday. He threw the paper on the man's desk and said "How dare you send me this! Don't you think I know what I owe?"

Still the landlord had things well enough arranged. He used to hunt two days a week and he kept his horse on one farm and put it to summer-grass on another. There was always someone willing. Sometimes he had a flutter in the market and bought a few store beasts. He could alwas find somewhere to send them for finishing.

By the time it came to the smoking of the pipes we and the majority were on our way back to the second milking. Some who had hands to leave things to would linger over shop-talk and a game of halfpenny nap. A few – like Charlie Elliott, who was a widower living with daughter and son-in-law – would make their way to the bar which they would be the last to leave.

By the time I had Quicksilver back in the shafts Mother would be there with her empty baskets. She never carried any of her shopping. We would mount up and tour round the shops she'd visited where they brought out the stuff and loaded it. The Old Man paid the bills and the Grocer always gave him a small cheroot.

When we were home and had milked and taken our

candles up to bed the landlord back at the Crown would end twelve hours of opening time by dealing with Charlie Elliott and his kind. The barman would shout out of the yard door to the ostler "Mr. Elliott's hoss!" They'd lead him out and lift him in and then the ostler would rattle his stick on the back of the cart. The pony would take him safely home – there were no motorcars on the road – when the family heard the cart come into the yard they would carry him indoors.

By then Old Glory would be somewhere over the landscape on the way to tomorrow's starting-place. Some years later he failed to turn up for duty and they found him dead in a ditch along one of the back tracks. His two dogs were beside him whining with hunger, unaware that a mile further down the green road were the rabbit snares he had set for feeding them.

They gave him a half-page obituary in the local paper. It was the first time we knew his name.

5
Feeding a Family

The English language is good on the subject of meat. Very definitive. It is not for nothing for instance that a pig when his throat is cut becomes pork; or a sheep that is knocked on the head becomes mutton. 'Pig' and 'sheep' are Saxon words. 'Pork' and 'Mutton' are Norman French. For many long years the serfs and villeins had the work of looking after animals that they seldom ate except as guests of their masters. They drove the Saxon ox that pulled the plough, but the Normans had first cut at the beef.

Even I can remember the ploughmen and carters and hedge-cutters being entertained by the Hunt at an annual Earth-stoppers' Dinner and passing up gleefully for second helpings. It was one of the two or three times a year that they tasted butcher's meat.

As far as the pig was concerned I believe things changed when the Tudor adventurers brought home the potato. It was then, I think, that it became possible for a cottager with only a quarter of an acre to keep a larger animal.

A stye was built down at the bottom corner and with homegrown pototoes, gleanings, household scraps, bakings done with mouldy flour and such things as hogweed gathered from the hedgerow it became possible for a family to feed one pig.

So it was until after the Second War. You could still hear the stye-pigs squealing at feeding-time. Then the bureaucrats brought in so many forms and rules about the movement of animals that the cottagers were parted from their pigs and the styes fell down. It was a sad parting. The yokel had a close relationship with the pig which is an amusing and companionable beast. As one old man said to me, "Dogs looks up to you. Cats looks down on you. But pigs is equal."

Equal or not, the time would come for killing the pig and that was a day of excitement. One man in the village held the honorary office of pig-killer in exchange for a contribution to his own larder and earned enough of such to make it unnecessary for him to keep a pig himself.

He arrived carrying an iron collar and chain with which his victim would be led up the garden path (so is language made!). A double iron hook with two pulleys was hung at full reach over a bough of the apple-tree and then all the family heaved on the ropes until the pig was hanging upside down. In this position he was killed and bled, then lowered onto a spread bale of straw and another one scattered over him. A match to the straw and all his bristles were soon singed off him, and the skin left ready for scraping.

Every bit of the pig was used – and as much as possible subjected to some form of preservation in those pre-freezing days. There were days of work for the cottage wife at pig killing, and for her neighbours who came to each others houses in turn to help.

The hams had to be pickled and made ready to be smoked in the chimney. Porkbelly was salted. The pig's head made brawn. The gut made the sausage-skins and the sausage-meat – made with trimmings and laced with pepper – was rammed down the skin tube with a broomhandle. There were chitterlings and trotters. They really did know how to use every bit of the pig but the squeak. In the latter times there came a new joke that said, "Now they've even found a use for the squeak. They're selling it to British Leyland for their brakes."

The pig, and the small flock of chicken that won most of their living scratching in the fields and hedges, gave a minimum supply of protein. Thus bacon and eggs became a standard English breakfast.

(It is to be noted that yokels do not say 'chickens'. For them, 'chicken' is the Saxon plural, like 'oxen'.)

For the rest the 10-rod cottage garden that could be seeded for a pound, made up a minimum diet for the family. It had to be cultivated on every free day of the year. Since everybody worked six days of the week and had to be at church Sunday mornings this amounted to Sunday afternoons and lighter evenings. It was easier earlier in history because there were innumerable Church holidays. Most of the old sayings about when crops should be planted or cultivated make reference to a Saint's Day.

In my earliest days there was still some gleaning and that meant a small supply of grain for which precious money need not be paid out. After each cornfield was harvested the cottage women waited for the signal. The last sheaf of corn was left standing in the field until the raking was done. A generous farmer might carry it out rightaway before the handrakes had been put in. Once the sheaf was gone the women and children went out to pick up every ear of corn that had been left lying there and the man would knock the grain out of them with his flail. You could take some of your gleaned sack to the mill to be ground for a few pence. But when I was born farm labourers were raising families on fourteen shillings a week. Much of the corn was eaten as whole grain in the form of frumenty.

'Frumenty' – called 'furmity' in some parts – was a pretty primitive food. It has been falsely glorified by two famous recipes – full of all kinds of meats and fruits and spices –

that have been often collected and published in books of Old English food. One of them, I believe actually refers to a banquet given by the Lord Mayor of London.

For cottage frumenty the grain was put in a three-legged iron pot half-full of water and left to stew and swell for hours in the ashes of the open fire. It was flavoured with salt or sugar and then supplemented with whatever could be had, sweet or savoury. Sometimes bacon scraps went into it, or the meat from pigs trotters, apples or the sharp fruit of the damson tree that grew in every cottage garden. In autumn they picked blackberries for the frumenty pot.

So, with a big clamp of potatoes that were shared with the pig, they had enough to eat. But, for a large part of the year, they were very short of protein.

As far as the search for protein was concerned the most important arrival in England was the rabbit.

Anyone who did not know the countryside before the 1950s could never imagine the number of rabbits in England at that time. Sometimes, walking down a lane on a summer evening and turning to look over the gate, it would be as if the whole strip of the field's edge, twenty or thirty yards wide, had turned brown and was moving towards the hedge.

The rabbit was probably a later import by the Normans. I believe there is no mention of it in Domesday Book. When it first came it was a surface, scrub-living animal and it made slow progress in the English climate. They kept it in enclosures that were walled around and dug with caves and tunnels to give protection – warrens. In these circumstances the rabbit gradually evolved into a burrowing creature. After that there was no stopping it.

The rabbits moved out into the banks and the hedgerows and dug underground tunnel-towns – called by us 'buries'

– which spread sometimes to a length of two furlongs, their passages snaking through the roots of the elm-trees.

The foxes ate them. The cats were always chasing them and bringing them into the house. The badgers dug the young ones out of the separate maternity holes that the females made at a distance from the main colony. The poorer people of the countryside relied on them.

Nobody needed to give me pocket-money because I was a professional rabbit hunter by the age of ten. Since I took from five to twenty-five of them to market every week – and they usually made sixpence each – I was a respectable contributor to the economy. Most country boys were educated early in the many skills of rabbit-catching. Purse-netting, long-netting, snaring, shooting and coursing. Each of them appropriate on its day.

Purse-netting is the highest form of rabbiting. A soft net of 2" mesh and about 30" diameter has a string threaded around its edge and tied to a sharpened hazel-stick. By pulling on the string you can draw the net up in just the same way as a sponge-bag. The net is used at the rabbits home site – the bury – and for a big bury many nets are needed since no single hole must remain uncovered. Working such a place three or four of us might use up to five dozen nets. There was never any shortage because each of us would spend many winter evenings with a netting needle and a 2" mesh-board, making them by lamplight.

On the other hand if you went on a long walk, and would be passing any number of small buries or just three or four holes, you could stuff half-a-dozen nets in one pocket and a ferret in the other. We often went to Chapel thus equipped because, knowing where everyone would be on that day, you could circle home by way of other folks' hedges and pick up a few rabbits while Mother got the Sunday dinner.

For such work we really needed Jim, the coney-dog, to sniff and tell us which holes were inhabited. Still he was always willing to doze on the Chapel steps until we had completed our devotions. We used to explain to people that he liked the singing. Those old coney-dogs were bred as a first cross between whippet and hunt-terrier. Bred pure the whippet lacked nose and brains while the terrier in his own right was not fast enough. As a first-cross they were very clever indeed and bursting with hybrid vigour.

The best of them were bred by a fellow called Old Luke, but it wasn't easy to buy one. He was very choosy about whose hands they were going to be in. The price was incidental – a shilling and a pint. Luke gave them good basic training before he passed them on and – as with all the old terrier-men – his only discipline was to whack them with his flat cap. A movement of his hand towards his cap brought instant obedience. If Jim was walking with you and you tipped your hat to a passer-by he would scuttle in close to heel.

The purse-nets are spread over every hole in the bury and the pegs pushed in alongside. This is done stealthily with only signs passing between the rabbiters. At this point the perfectionist will sit silent for a quarter-hour at least, allowing the rabbits to forget the disturbance before the ferrets are put in through the nets. Thus their minds are not divided between two anxieties, above and below.

As the ferrets work their way through the tunnels they must smell to the rabbit like the stoat, the ferret's wild cousin which is the rabbits most feared enemy. This slim, fierce little creature could never run down a rabbit above ground, but he can creep through the tunnels to which they run to avoid their other enemies. From the stoat or the ferret there is no escape except to bolt for the open, and that leads straight to the nets.

As a rabbit tangles in the net the rabbiter's hand is on it in a second and in two seconds its neck is broken. Properly done it is quick and quite humane. Nothing arouses the scorn of other rabbiters more than messing up this part of the action – unless it be missing a pop-hole when the nets are laid.

The geography of a rabbit bury will always include, among the obvious burrows, two or three concealed exits hidden usually under a bramble, a thistle-patch or a pile of leaves. These narrow pop-holes are only half opened up. When danger threatens and there has been disturbance at the main entrances a rabbit will often quietly open one up and creep through the undergrowth until he makes open ground and can bolt away.

When the nets are laid it is best for each man to carry a fagging-hook, switching aside the brambles and rubbish to locate the hidden pop-holes. If he misses one it will be on his section that the rabbits get away. If they do, then it may be the coney-dog who will save his face. During the ferreting Jim used to sit back silently twenty yards from the bury. His bright eyes scanned backwards and forwards along the bank. Sometimes he would himself be watched by an apprentice dog whose lead had been pegged to the ground with a garden fork.

Jim would spot a creeping rabbit instantly and watch until it was committed to the open; then he shot out like a silent arrow. He would be back with it in a minute, growling a warning to his pupil as he put it down.

Long-netting was quite a different matter and never took place without the Old Man, who considered that it required his supervision. He had a special old coat for the purpose

– a black coat with a fly-front. Nothing can bring disaster
to long-netting like exposed buttons. The thing has just
about the dimensions of a tennis-court net but is a hundred
yards long. Lines are threaded through top and bottom
that are shorter than the net itself by several yards; thus
when it is set it hangs very loose and baggy. The whole
thing was kept in folds about the length of a broomstick
that hung in the woodshed.

I still have our net – which we acquired in comic circumstances – but nowadays rabbits exist almost nowhere
in numbers that justify the use of it. In fact, the method
is largely forgotten. That is my excuse for putting long-netting
on the record in detail. It should be remembered that what
follows had to be performed in pitch darkness and dead
silence.

At the end of the summer when the young were well-
grown the big buries would be very crowded. The rabbits
had to work more and more out into the field and the
further they went the more nervous and alert they became.

At this season the Old Man checked the weather each
night after supper. There would now and then come a
pitch-dark evening with a strong noisy wind, then he
would decide there was a chance to slide the net between
the feeding rabbits and their burrows.

The netting team would walk quickly down to the gate
of the chosen field and, holding the two ends of the
broomstick, pass the net over. We had also an old army
kit-bag in which were the thirty stakes – yard-long hazels
with a point at one end and a notch at the other – on which
it was to be hung.

With only the vague black shadow of the hedge on my
left I would creep along and push the pegs in – one for
every three of my small paces. The Old Man followed,

peeling the net off its stick and pushing the top-line into the notches at just the right tension. All this without disturbing the feeding rabbits out in the field. By the same token, the others, the beaters, had to creep along two other hedges, and end up on the opposite side of the field facing towards us. When the net was set we would squat on our heels each a quarter way from the end. Thus we had half the net each to manage as we sat holding the top line in our finger-tips.

Now the night was split by a piercing whistle from the Old Man. The time for silence had gone. We wanted the rabbits on their feet and bolting for home. We heard the beaters begin to whistle and call in turn as they worked towards us, dragging their lines between them. These lines, which they had unrolled as they took their places, were tied every yard with bunched-up newspapers that rustled as it came over the grass, checking any rabbit that tried to run back and scaring up those that had followed the instinct to squat in face of danger. As the rabbits hit the net we felt the line shake and had to get to each quickly while he dangled and dispatch him properly.

It was enthralling. I can remember every night of long-netting I ever had. Our best ever bag was fifty-six rabbits in one drive. Fourteen dinners for a big family. Twenty-eight shillings in the market – and that in the late Twenties was exacty a week's wages for a farm-hand. But often we came home with nothing at all. Somebody just had to trip over a twig.

I found our long-net against the Close hedge at daybreak one morning when I went out to get the cows in. Someone had set it and then just left it. Ten years later I finished a pint in the Royal Oak one Autumn evening and announced that I was going long-netting. "Ah" said an old lad in the corner, "with my bloody net." He had taken a drink or two and let out his secret. I asked him how it happened. "Well" he said, "I wasn't going to face the Old Man. I heard the gate rattle and looked up and saw him there 'count of his white milking-coat he was wearing. So I legged it."

At home we worked out that the Old Man had not gone out that night but that Quicksilver, the old white pony, had been turned out in the next field. She liked a bit of company and used to rattle the gate to get your attention. She must have known the rabbiting man was there and decided she'd like a word.

It must have been a sore loss to the old lad because it was a real poacher's net, made of fine silk thread so that the whole length of it could be stuffed into a small bag. They say he could work it by himself with just his dog to quarter the ground and drive the rabbits to him. When the Old Man died I went to give it back to him, but he too had passed away.

The other ways of getting rabbits didn't interest us much, though we could practise them if necessary.

Snaring is unpleasant. There is a feeling of murder about the way it slowly strangles the victim leaving it lying with its head swollen up and distorted. It was used chiefly for the sly taking of rabbits in forbidden places. A man going home at sunset would set a few wires – each held hand-high with a peg and a twig halfway between the jumps in a rabbit run – and hope to find a brace when he passed again in the morning. If you were willing to cut your pegs on the spot you could secrete a dozen wires, each in a little coil, undetectable about your person. But I would have been ashamed to take snared rabbits to market.

It is possible to shoot a rabbit so that none of the pellets strike behind the shoulder. Sometimes. With a bit of luck. But mostly they get knocked about and filled with shot. We might take the gun only if somebody said at short notice "Go and get a rabbit for dinner."

Worst of all were the big rabbit shoots. They were something to be stayed away from.

They would choose a big bury, usually in a wood, and put the ferrets in without netting. Once all the rabbits were driven out in the open the holes were stuffed with newspaper dipped in tar and creosote. Rather than try and get home past that the fastidious rabbits would lie out all night in the undergrowth. Next day everyone who could lay hands on a gun, together with all their dogs, came along to scare them up and shoot them.

I have known two dogs shot on such an occasion, and more than one man severely peppered. The Old Man used to say he'd been shot at by the Boers and he'd rather face that than a line of mixed rabbit-shooters.

Coursing rabbits was something for little boys with time on their hands. The grass on the slopes where the land climbed up to the heath was dotted with briar patches and there we went with our Jim and the neighbour's spaniel – a real professional pair.

The rabbits grazing the slopes would bolt into the patches when they were disturbed and we set out to bolt them forth again. Jim disdained to risk his skin in such places but the spaniel would push in as soon as he caught a scent. As he ploughed through the prickles the coney-dog would circle the outside like a scrum-half, his eyes shining. When the rabbit made a bolt for it he had about a hundred yards to go to the next patch. Jim would pick him up by halfway. It was a lot of walking for one or two rabbits, but great fun for dogs and boys.

Oh, for the days of the rabbits. Up on the poor hill holdings they relied on them for living. You'd see the market-cart going in with ash-poles laid across on which were hung tightly packed pairs – the rabbits legged by nicking behind one hamstring and tucking the other leg through.

I think the gods got rid of the small country people and their favourite free dinner all in one planned operation. In two decades a quarter of a million farm hands were made redundant and replaced by machines. Their cottages went to the retired people, the weekenders, the executives who motor twenty-five miles to the industrial estate, the computer consultant who sits in the old parlour and communicates electronically.

And in one decade the Myxy disease killed ninety per cent of the rabbits in England.

They should put a cross in the churchyard:-

In Memory of
RABBIT PIE
1300 – 1953
and of
Hodge and his Family

page 51
file 138

6
The Sacred Horses

We had two kinds of horses and our lives depended on them. In truth, life had depended on horses since the Iron Age when Boudicca and her warriors worshipped Epona the Goddess of the Foals.

This horse-worship came late in human history. For ages horses were for a man a source of food. The Stone Age caves had piles of horse bones that had been split to get out the marrow.

It was when the horse went to war that he rose to his distinction. The mounted peoples swept the World. Thenceforward every statue of a great man was on horseback. I remember after the Kaiser's War when they put Earl Haig up in Whitehall the better papers concentrated on criticising the horse. The cavalier contempt for those who are restricted to Shanks's Pony is still to be detected in places where there is a strong smell of horses.

Since the usefulness of the horse died away he has been sustained by his symbolism. The majority of the horses now in Britain are owned by those who feel they are carried on his back to some distinction.

And nobody in England would eat him; though the Englishman abroad may sometimes wonder about the yellowness of fat and slight sweetness of taste in his 'carbonade de boeuf'. In England the hunter who goes incurably lame is sent not to the horse-butcher but to the hunt kennels where he is consumed by the hounds he spent his life following.

But, as I said, the prime moving power of our lives was provided by horses and much of our thought was devoted to them. The Old Man used to say, "What shall we talk about or horses?"

We also had an uncle who said "What shall we do, or go fishing?" But that's another story.

Our two kinds of horses had separate quarters. Down by the old yard were the cart stables and up by the green – Mother's drying ground where the broody coops stood in the Spring – were the nag stables. Each had four stalls and a loose-box at each end, one of which was used as a feed-house. Down the whole length ran a manger made of elm coffin-boards with rings through which the halter ropes went held taut by their swinging wooden clogs. Above, a long rack made of ash-poles held the hay that we pushed down through holes in the floor of the loft.

On the door-wall the horse tack hung on wooden tree crutches chosen and cut when we were firewooding.

George Morland painted stables like this. Years later in a Kensington drawing room I saw his 'In the Stable'. It took me a moment to grasp that it was the original. Quite a small picture but worth more than all our farm. Nowadays his pictures hang in places like this but they were painted in places like ours. The big horses rattle their clogs as they feed, rolling an eye back to check on the playing children. The hens scratch in the straw. A pig wanders in to see if there's anything going.

We climbed up the stall boards and clambered on their backs. Slid down their hind legs with a tight grip on the tail. We crawled under their bellies and none of them would ever put a 14lb foot on us.

On the wall hung various old tools of horse-doctoring. Every carter did most of his own. The twitch-stick with a loop of thick rope that could be twisted on his nose to keep him steady. The big rasp for taking the sharp edges off his teeth when a horse was eating uneasily and his tongue looked swollen. The drenching horn, taken from a four year old bullock and hollowed through, with which you could pour medicine down past his tongue.

In the cupboard on the wall was the famous embrocation for sprains for which every horse man had his secret recipe. And the hoof oil. And there also lay grandfather's old fleam, like a horn-hardened penknife with three heart-shaped blades. Beside a thick short ebony stick. He was always ready to give a discourse on how it was done even though, in his old age, he couldn't believe they ever could have done such a thing. You twisted a cord tourniquet round a limb until a main vein swelled up. Then you set the chosen size of blade against it and whacked it with the fleam stick. Thus every waggoner knew how to bleed his horses in the days when men were bled for almost every ailment.

I still have the fleam together with a big poultice boot that hung from the stable beam – a big soft leather bag with a drawstring and an oak sole. Into this the horse's foot was put, smothered with a hay mash made with Jeyes Fluid, when he'd run his foot on a nail and there were signs of festering.

With it all there were few ailments and, considering the desperate power they were called on to apply in difficult situations – very few accidents to the horses.

We did suffer once for lending a horse to the big house. The gardener borrowed a mare just before haytime to pull the mower in Home Park, and managed to run her into a fencing stake all down one side.

The Old Man sewed her up with gut from my fishing-box

and a sack needle, then went off to market to buy something cheap to get us out of trouble.

The horse he came back with was a sight to see. Tall
and thin with long swinging legs that finished in frying-pan
feet. A great coffin head with a huge wolf tooth sticking
out of his mouth.

It was clear that he'd had trouble tackling his grub, so
the vet came and doped him with Chloral Hydrate. Four
of us held him against the stable wall while he heaved out
the monstrous molar with a big pair of pinchers. Within
a couple of days he was eating with a will.

The Old Man couldn't scarcely bear to look at him – and
was very keen that no-one should catch sight of him – so
he was handed over to me for the side-rake and the swathe-
turner which were the boys' tools at haytime. He did a
good job and I got on very well with him. The only other
person who regarded him with affection was a pig.

She herself was an outlaw. An old sow who wouldn't
come into the buildings and had her pigs down in the
hedgerows. It was never very safe to go near her but she
came snorting up for her food at the rattle of a bucket.
Every so often we drove her into the float and carted her
over to the boar next door. I think that even he was nervous
of her.

The first time I drove the market-horse out to work she
came out of the double-hedge to meet him, pushed up her
snout and snorted at him. For the rest of that haytime she
walked with him up every row of every field, turned every
corner with him, lay down beside him when he had his
nosebag at 'baver' time. At night she went with us as far
as the yard and in the morning met us at the field gate. It
was an uncommunicative but romantic association.

When the season ended and the good mare was healed

the Old Man sold him cheap to a higgler who used to work the district. He had a bargain. For years afterwards when they came to our place – offering something the higgler had found or delivering something we'd asked him to find – the Old Horse always knew me.

Apart from accidents the working horses were always very well and this, of course, was the product of the fine art of horse feeding.

You'll get no idea of what working horses looked like from the heavy horses you see in the ring nowadays – poor zoo animals that they now are, and some of them looking more like hippos. When I see some of them prancing under the floodlights I remember that you could stop your pair anywhere along a row and walk over to the hedge to look at a bird's nest. You knew they would never move a foot but stand there thanking the Lord that work had stopped for a precious moment.

You'd never see any fat on a working horse any more than you would on a boxer. Their muscles were all separated and defined, like those you see on the back of a heavy-weight as he strips out in the ring. Horses were fed exactly to the work they were doing and only a good carter knew how to do it. He was as accurate in his catering as the diesel engine pump that spits into the cylinder measures exactly the fuel that is needed to produce a certain speed.

Hard horse hay was chaffed up with the best straw and mixed in the round cane sieve with chosen quantities of cracked field beans and maize. Occasionally a few handfuls of oats. Then on Sunday, the day of rest, the rations were cut right back – just hay and perhaps a bran-mash made with a bit of boiled linseed. Neglect of this meant that the horses would come out of their rest day dopey and idle. This was called Monday Morning Disease and was the sign of a man who didn't know his job.

It was their management of the prime source of working energy that set the carters apart as the aristocrats among farm workers. Twenty-seven shillings a week they earned, and a new whip every third Michaelmas, when the dairy men were getting fourteen shillings.

They were proud and distinctly haughty. Old Jim Hines would dismiss anyone else's opinion with just the words, 'I'm the horse man'. When he was very old and lame he had two horses lying out in the furthest field at haytime. When Horace, the dairyman, got up at sunrise he saw the horses were standing at the gate and, meaning to be helpful, went over and caught them. He brought them down riding one and his belt around the neck of the other.

Later Jim limped into the yard in a panic. "I lorst my bloody osses" he said, and Horace told him they were already in the stable. Without a word Jim haltered them up and led them all the way back again, turned them out and drove them over the far side. Then he caught them, and led them all the way back again. "I'm the horse man on this farm," he said.

Apart from horse management and the skill of ploughing, the Carter looked after the breeding, and the breaking and training of young stock. At the County Show in the summer he was there to look over the sires and make up his mind who should go on his mares, returning home with a pocketful of stallion cards to pin up in the stable.

Next spring each stallion offered for breeding would go on his travels. As it was said, he went walking. He would stride down the lanes for weeks on end all dressed up in his ribbons, led by a tiny little man wearing polished gaiters. It was the custom to have a horse walked by the smallest man who could manage him. It made the horse look even bigger.

I well remember the big horses on the road, and the carters leading their mares on to the pubs and farms for which standing dates had been announced on the stallion cards. But – although early on I drove a shire called Captain who was born of one of these assignations – by the time I was ready for man's work the Old Man had done a deal that meant no more heavy horses were born on our place.

In our market town there was a family that ran what would nowadays be called a trucking-fleet. In those days road transport was horse work and in their stables there were no less than forty heavies. All of them were Suffolk Punches, the great chestnut horses that had less feather on their legs and a faster walking pace than a Shire. They came from East Anglia where they had descended from the Dutch horses brought over for the draining of the Fens.

The Old Man had been at school with the son of this business and every year it took the best hay we had for sale and tons of the power-packing horse beans that we grew. There were carts and road waggons enough to keep a wheelwright in full-time business and a lad who filled his whole time looking after harness. He used to throw whole sets of it in a bath of oil with a lamp burning under it. It was neatsfoot oil, in obedience to the old rule – mineral on mineral, vegetable on vegetable and animal on animal. So it was mineral oil on engines, linseed oil on woodwork and, on the leather, neatsfoot made by boiling up the hooves at the slaughterhouse 'Neats' is the old English name for cattle.

The waggons from that place – and from the other hauliers – were to be seen on the move everywhere. They carried the bricks and the coal and the timber and every other heavy load that came to the railway yards. The work was hard and cruel. It was amazing the heart with which

the horses did it. Charging into their collars and stamping
their toes in to hold the loads on the steep hills. Sometimes
in deep mud, sometimes on iron hard cobbles. In three
years the road teams ended up work-shy and with the
joints of their legs shaken. Every year more three-year-olds
came over from East Anglia; and every year the Old Man
took three or four off the hard roads – all of them mares
– and turned them out in our soft fields for recovery.

After a year's rest in the country the Punch mares were
back to top form – sound and lively and willing. So it was
that almost all the work I ever did was with them. I loved
them very much. And so it was also that the farmers of
our district came to establish a splendid line in heavyweight
hunters.

Our landlord at that time owned a blood horse that had
won a Classic race and farmers whom he favoured were
each allowed to put two or three working mares a year to
it. The first cross between the clean-limbed Punch mare
and the thoroughbred produced a splendid saddle-horse,
full of quantity, and well up to the fifteen stone or more
that was quite common among the overweight gentlemen
who were members of the smart Hunt down in the Vale.
From then on there was always at least one animal that
was being got ready for that market.

Most of the time though we were driving the mares to
work. And, of course, apart from an occasional road journey
to load a cart with coal, we drove them almost always on
foot. Those heavies you see at shows nowadays being
driven coachman-style are in road-waggons that belonged
to brewers and the millers.

With a cart we walked beside a single horse holding his
halter. With a pair side by side we drove them in chains,
not with reins but with rope lines. It must be thirty years

since I saw a set of plough-lines for sale at the saddlers. If I ever saw another set I would buy them just as a keepsake. They were about fourteen feet long and not level like other ropes. At a point about two thirds along their length they tapered up and down again to form a thick piece that hung just alongside the horse's hip on each side. These were for communication, and they worked like a rider's heel. Swinging them in a circle you could give a sharp tap either side. Wobbling them up and down or shaking them you could have a variety of what an equestrian would call 'aids'.

When two or even three horses were needed to pull a farm load they were worked in line ahead. One horse went in the shafts wearing a working version of the famous back-pad 'Thil' harness that you now see parading in such highly decorated form. 'Thil', by the way, is an old word for shafts. You hooked the next horses in front of him with the plough chains.

You walked forward of the near front wheel – against which incidentally the waggoner was allowed legally to relieve himself in order that his team remained under control. You held the halter of the Thiller and the lines from the chain-horse, together with sometimes the long, brass bound whip that rested back over your right shoulder. Thus you walked every yard your horses went. That's why there are so many little waggoner's pubs along the English lanes – some of them still preserving their whip racks over the fireplace. You were glad to sit down for a pint when the time came for the horse to take their nose-bags.

A tug of the halter. A tap with the lines. Sometimes a touch of the whip. Yet with all these the most important driving aid was the voice, and carters talked continually to their horses.

To begin with every horse knew his name and recognized

whether an instruction was for him particularly. Secondly, a trained horse had a very large vocabulary. To make a horse forward, for instance, we said 'Gitton', not 'Gee up' which in our parts meant 'turn right'. To turn right more sharply was 'Gee Back'. To the near side it was 'Comee' and 'Come back'. So, with 'Steady' and 'Gittover' and a dozen others, the lines and the halter were often slack and only called on for precise manoeuvres.

I once enjoyed an unforgettable excitement on market day when I was a boy. Out of the Crown Tap tumbled a raucous group of waggoners obviously all set for a lark. One of their number, in his cups, had wagered that he would drive his four horse waggon anywhere in the town with the reins removed.

They lifted him up on his seat, unbuckled the reins and climbed in the back, with me up over the tailboard to join them. The men in the back sat quiet – they all knew horses – and just one of them called out instructions for the route. Thus we set off through the busy old market town, and you know the geography of such places.

With 'Gee Captain' and 'Gittover Joe' and 'Comee Jane' we made our way. We did knock a chip out of the corner of the solicitor's office and did irreparable damage to a barrowload of chicken crates that had been left unattended. But he made it. The news went right round the town and as he returned the market emptied as people came up to cheer him back to the Tap.

Armed with the rudiments of all this know-how at the age of twelve we might be sent out to the fields to bring back a two-horse waggon loaded with four ton of hay. It was scary but we did it. It was particularly scary if we got landed with the quarter-lock waggon.

You will have noticed that the waggons you see driven

in the show-ring nowadays almost always have small front wheels that can be turned on a lock right under the back of the vehicle. This provides remarkable manouverability. But on the soil of many farms these small wheels would sink in the mud. So some farm-waggons were built with big wheels front and back. The front wheels, even on a special wide axle, could be turned less than a quarter of a circle before colliding with the side of the waggon. This meant that you had to judge your route so that it followed a series of wide curves. It was a phenomenon I met later in life when driving a Churchill tank in its higher gears.

You had to get your approach to the gate exactly right – and that with horses stretching their powers to the full. If you came round too wide you'd end up nose to the hedge. That might mean shutting out your horses and hitching on behind with just two sets of chains to pull back and get another start. If you came round too narrow the wheel could touch the waggon and you could end up with four ton of hay on top of you.

More than fifty years later I still sometimes dream about the quarter-lock. At that age – when nowadays the law would not even allow you to take a ride on someone else's tractor trailer – it was a nightmare.

7
A Step So Jolly

Apart from an occasional hunter in temporary residence, or the odd pony that the boys were working on with an eye to middle-class children's market, our Nag Stables were occupied by the Cobs, beloved partners of the Yeoman of England – small farmers, small traders and small craftsmen – for centuries. They are the middle weights. Strong enough to work in farm machinery. Active and sturdy under the saddle. Supreme as a trotting road-horse in the days before motorcars.

Britain has the best cobs in the world – nobody would deny it – and each of the three most prominent strains shows a touch of exotic blood mixed with that of the original native ponies. In the Highlander, whom you have seen in prints and paintings, carrying the stags down off the hill, a touch of Norse blood that shows in the stripes on his back and ankles. In the Fells the jet black colour and luxurious mane and tail contributed by Dutch horses brought over from East Anglia. In the Welsh cobs, it is said, the earliest touch of Arabic blood that was brought here by Roman colonial cavalry and can be seen particularly in the face.

The Old Man's love was for our native Fells and no-one had a closer understanding with them. In the old days in our district their special job had been pack-horse work, bringing the lead ore down from the mines in the hills. Twelve black cobs in line all tied nose to tail each carrying two pannier boxes with a hundredweight of ore on each side. They needed sure feet on the hill paths and great self-control. One of the pack-men used to have a collie dog that ran with them. At points where the hill came down one side so that it bumped the panniers but fell away in a precipice on the other side, the dog used to run up and down the line snapping at the heels of any horse that strayed too near the edge. It was journeys like this three times a day that sorted out the best and founded the virtues of the breed.

The Fell cobs were born up on the exposed tops of the hills and lived their first two years exposed to severe weather. Then they came down to spend a winter in the yard – all together like bullocks – with racks of hay and troughs of cracked oats mixed with barley. This way they really grew.

Next Spring the Old Man would start on them one at a time. The young cob would be put in a Yorkshire halter – which unlike other halters has a throat-lash – and the end of it tied to a long cart rope. The rope was then passed through a swivelled iron ring cemented in the centre of the outer yard.

The horse would get off round the yard and was encouraged to go. Soon three or four of us on the other end of the rope would pull him in to the centre of the yard and hold him with his nose over the ring. This was repeated often and soon the horse would start to come to the centre as soon as he felt the pressure. Once the Old Man found that he could pull the horse with just his own weight he would send the rest of us away and carry on alone. Soon he had tied the long rope to the ring and walked up to start controlling the horse with the halter. He understood an individual horse so quickly, and was so good at putting ideas into their heads, that he had been known to start on one in the morning and be driving it in harness by supper-time.

The Old Man used to say that the training and management of horses is based on teaching them one big lie – that a man is stronger than a horse. This is what he was doing with his cart-rope tactics.

The gypsies – who are wonderfully talented with horses – start each horse by pulling him right down with a rope; and you will have seen in films the cowboys doing it, four or five men on the end of a rope. I suppose that what used to be called 'breaking' a horse is really an act of brain-washing.

There is a belief nowadays that horses should not be broken but schooled. That the whole process should be gentle from the beginning so that the horse is not fooled about a man's strength but just never put in the position of discovering that he himself is about ten times the stronger. The trouble is that later on, in a crisis or in the hands of an uncertain rider, he may make the discovery and then he can become unmanageable. When he does some people are apt to get very angry with him. The Old Man never got angry with horses.

It's better for a horse to learn the big lie because he'll carry it with him all his life. Horses do not have the conceptual intelligence of men, or the undoubted reasoning power of a dog, but they have the world's best memories.

An uncle of ours who used to visit now and again once drove over with a young horse and just as he got close a white hen ran squawking out of the hedge and put the horse in a terrible fright. Four years later when he came again with the same, now experienced road-horse it shied right across the road at the point where the chicken had run out.

An old fishing friend of mine who had been in the cavalry told me that they loaded their horses at Bulford Camp and set off for a seven year posting to India. By the time they returned the whole regiment had been remounted but for four horses. When they unloaded at Bulford those four horses each walked straight to his own proper stall.

The Fell horses are fewer now – though they've had a bit of a new lease with pony-trekking – but when I see them in the show ring it brings back all the old days. For myself, when I was very young I fell in love with the Welshmen, originally one particular Welshman called Tony who for years was more a brother than a horse. I met him when he was three years old and he lived to over thirty.

When the roads were still McAdam flint and not yet Tarmacadamed, the Welsh small farmers who reared their cobs on the hills of Cardigan used to drive them into England every year. They had done so for centuries, coming out through Monmouth and on past Gloucester. From one market town to another they went, following the country roads and the old green droves, resting and feeding them on the commons that were still unenclosed. After a week or two on the trail they travelled quietly in a close herd. Up on the green roads we used to pick up the flat, leaf-shaped eighteenth-century horse-shoes that had been dropped by the ponies ridden by the men who wrangled them across the land. Still today one of the Welshmen brings his mountain ponies every year to the horse-fair at Stow-in-the-Wold – but nowadays in cattle-waggons.

We bought Tony in our local market when the very last drove was at the end of the trail. I think that all that were left were sold that day and then the Welshmen trotted back home never to come again on horseback.

Three-year-old and unbroken he cost £6, including a new halter. It was the custom then that the price of a horse always included a halter.

We decided it was best to take him home by the green tracks rather than round by the turnpike. Every few yards he stopped and pricked up his ears, gazing round the landscape. He whinnied every time he noticed something that might be evidence of another horse. He kept trying to wheel round in front of me because he'd been driven so far and couldn't get used to leading. But he was good and kind – and I lost my heart to him because he kept looking at me as if to ask what was going to happen to him.

So many things happened to him and me. We learned so many things together, some of which the Old Man considered would have been best left unlearned.

Having the misfortune to be the middle brother it was my duty after morning milking – while the others went to breakfast and mine went in the oven – to take the churns of milk down to the turnpike to meet the lorry. Thousands of times Tony and I made that journey in the old market-cart. Once the churns were loaded we turned for home.

Every driving pony puts on a bit of a spurt when his head turns towards home. You are supposed to control it and make sure that he travels with proper style and dignity in all directions. But Tony and I shared a single purpose – home and breakfast. The journey back to the farm in the unloaded cart developed into a daily chariot-race.

I rode him over the fields to count sheep or move bullocks and in the end at this latter job I just had to sit and watch. Once I'd shown him which bullock we wanted to cut out he would turn it and head it and swing across to turn it again – just like a cattle-dog. If one moved a bit too slowly for him, he'd bite it on the backside.

A long time later at a well-known equestrian establishment I saw a demonstration of the famous American 'cutting-horses' doing just the same thing. They were greatly applauded. Personally I thought they didn't do it quite as well as Tony. I never realised that what I had all those years ago was a 'cutting horse'.

I also trained him as a dragoon horse. That is to say, I could fire a gun from the saddle. It took a long time, starting off firing the gun a long way from him when he was feeding and gradually getting closer. In the end he would stand rock-steady when he was warned that it was coming. The rabbits took a lot less notice of you when you came quietly along on horse-back. The deer are the same. But although I could get rabbits from his back I could never bring them home. He couldn't stand the smell of a dead rabbit close to him. I had to take him home and then walk all the way back to pick up the bag.

We had a day's hunting together now and again and once a year the hunting people used to give us a special job to do. A number of the leading members of the Hunt also used to keep bloodhounds and held an annual trial. The secretary picked out Tony and me because we knew the country and it was our job to lay the scent, what is called 'the drag'. From the starting point we were told which area to cover and given a place to finish. They didn't give us much time and it wouldn't be long before we heard the hounds behind us.

The drag was a noisome thing. It was a sack half-full of sheep's guts and ferret's nests and fox droppings and aniseed. Anything that would make a smell. It bounced along behind us on a rope tied round a stirrup leather. The blood hounds never had any trouble with it and came on fast. We dragged it through quarries and up the beds of streams but it never seemed to check them.

We were the centre of attention that day and got cheered as we came in ahead of the hounds. They also used to pass the cap round – "For the Drag, ladies and gentlemen!"

The Old Man used to be quite proud of us on that day. Anyway, he was in favour of youngsters getting out and earning a bob or two.

It was a different matter if Quicksilver was lame and he had to take Tony to market. As he struggled to bring him back gently from the turnpike he used to curse me and say I wasn't to be trusted with horses.

It was one day that I was brushing Tony down ready for the laying of the drag that – impressed by the company I was about to keep and stirred by the smart horses I had seen in the hunting-field – I took the sheep shears and set out to clip his heels clean. Just as I had done it, the Old Man walked in and I don't think I ever saw him so angry. It frightened me. "You've ruined the horse" he said. Looking at Tony, who was himself peering round sheepishly at his own heels, I realised he was right. A cob must always have a little bit of feathers as any lover of the sort will tell you. It ruined my day and I waited longingly for his heels to grow out again.

If you live with Welsh Cobs when you are young you will love them the rest of your days. Their contribution to horse history is very great.

When Sir Galahad – or any other Knight of Chivalry – rode out on his stylish palfrey his squire rode behind on a Welsh cob, leading the great warhorse that was loaded with the arms and armour. The palfrey was trained to a gentle ambling pace for the comfort of ladies and gentlemen and bishops. The cob was a trotter – and today the road trot is still his best pace.

The Welsh cob emigrated to America and, crossed with the Spanish horses from Mexico – founded the Western cow-pony. There is also little doubt that America's top-class driving horse, the Morgan, is descended in line from an imported Welsh stallion.

Thousands of Welsh Cobs died in the Kaiser's War with the Royal Horse Artillery, pulling the famous 18-pounder guns of which now just one troop still exists for the firing of royal salutes.

George Bowanan the great driving champion – and partner in sport of the Duke of Edinburgh – founded his reputation on a team of Welshcobs. At the time I write he is training a new Championship team of black Welsh.

They have been crossed very effectively with the British Commoner. The Commoner is an ancient, sturdy and somewhat coarsely-made breed of which I think the true origin is not known. They are best known to the public for pulling the gypsies' waggons. They are almost always what we called 'coloured horses' though some talk about piebald and skewbald. In fact, there are four colours. Black and white, brown and white and the Blagdons which are roan and white. Blagdon is a village in Somerset but I don't know how they got the name. There are 'blue Blagdons' and 'strawberry Blagdons', patched with blue and red respectively.

Gypsies have always loved coloured horses and so have Red Indians. I think it is because both races are well familiar with horse stealing. After all, if a bay horse or a chestnut horse is stolen in the South of England you would be hard put to prove it was the same animal if it turned up in Yorkshire – unless it was branded. There is no mistaking a coloured horse. Every one has a pattern exclusive to himself and can be picked out anywhere.

Anyway, it is with the commoners that the Welsh cob has been used to produce the beautiful coloured cobs that the costers bring every year to the International Horse

Show. And they are to be seen in more distinguished places. This year at the gypsy Horse Fair at Appleby there was a royal official looking to buy young coloured horses to carry the drums of the Household Cavalry.

To be honest there is one thing about the Welsh cobs which in some cases amounts to a fault, and it was this particularly that kept the Old Man faithful to his Fells. It is the tendency among some to breed them with a very high knee action.

This action started first in East Anglia, where the roads were bad and the fields were deep in winter mud. Here a horse had to pull his feet up out of the mire at every pace, and one with a high up-and-down action got on better. Later it was equated with style and became a fashion. It is still to be seen today at its full absurdity in the Hackney Classes at horse shows.

Some of our farmers liked the style. They were the ones who wanted to put on a show on Market Day; and indeed it was a show worth seeing. They drove corned-up young ponies which went beautifully but nevertheless gave a feeling that they would take off without hesitation in the wrong hands. The market-carts were as smart as Liverpool gigs and built on the same style. The tack glistened. These turn-outs were the sports cars of their day.

Charley Elliott's turn-out was one of the best and he drove his hot little horses beautifully even though he'd usually had a couple of drinks. I lovingly remember the day when he entertained the market at the expense of a young policeman.

This constable – new to the district – strode out as Charley was driving down the High Street singing himself a song. He took hold of the bridle and said, "Now Sir, I'm taking you in charge for being drunk in charge of a horse vehicle."

"Quite right" said Charlie. "Drunk I am. You get up alongside me and I'll drive us to the station." Not seeing any other way out of it the policeman did so,

Fifty yards further on Charley stopped "Dammit," he said "I said I'd get my wife some stewing steak. Here, hang on to him," and he disappeared into the butchers. After watching the resulting scene through the window until there appeared to be real danger to the general traffic he came out again. "Well, well, well! Fancy a big man like you letting a little 'oss play you up. Here, give to me."

A little further on he stopped again. "Oh my Lord" he said, "I forgot the fish. Hang on to him" and he made for the fishmongers. When he came out the horse was tied to a lamp-post and the policeman had disappeared.

Charley liked his horses with a nice high action, and despite the splendour of his display the Old Man would eye it disparagingly, saying "He's got a right knees-upper there."

The Old Man liked those that reached out long at the trot. "Give me a cob that trots like a cat" he used to say. This love of a horse that could point its toe was left over from the time when they used to race their ponies on the road after Chapel every Sunday. In my earliest days they were still doing it.

A mile up the road from the pub opposite the churchyard was a post. That's where they started from, racing a measured mile. A man with a big white flag could be seen waving it from the pub door and so with a good old turnip watch they achieved accurate timing without benefit of any electrics. For two hours before dinner the men made their challenges to one another, encouraged by side-betting friends. Despite the sanctity of the day there was a good deal of sinful wagering and it had been known for a man to bet his horse against another and lose it. The other fellow gave it back to him, said it wasn't worth having. It only came in three seconds behind.

As each man came down a queue of others would be moving quietly up the other side of the track so you could always hear the clatter of the next one on the way. Most of them raced in their carts but a few came down in the saddle. This was the older way. When they were in the carts they were 'osses', but under saddle they always called them 'gallowas' which was an old word that came down from the Border horse-sales.

Well into my great-grandfather's time there were almost no roads in England except the main turnpikes that were fit for vehicles in wintertime. It was only after McAdam that the coachbuilders started to build the light horse vehicles that were brought to such perfection. Before that what was needed was a saddle roadster that would keep a good pace across miles of country with a big man on his back. The best of them were bred in Norfolk. Some of them became famous.

Readers of George Borrow will remember that while the Romany Rye was first at Lincoln Horse Fair with the Petulengros there was a sudden hush among the people. An old man came leading a very old horse through the crowd. Farmers, gypsies, dealers, they all raised their hats and Petulengro said to him "When you're an old man you can tell your grandbabbies that you saw Marshland Shales." Shales, I have been told, did twenty miles within the hour when he was over twenty years old.

Another famous horse among the roadsters was the mare Silvertail. She belonged to the great horse-artist John Herring and he travelled the land with her in a gig, carrying his clothes and his paints, and stopping at one after another of the great houses to paint their hunters and racehorses and dogs. Wherever he went he challenged the district to road-racing and is said to have made a tidy bit by it. He'd need to because in those days he was treated rather as an upper servant and stayed in the servants' hall. Today, of course, any one of his pictures would buy you a big house.

Herring's son, Ben who followed his father's craft, did a print of Silvertail under saddle just coming up to the post in a road-trial. It's on my wall.

The London costermongers were great lovers of cobs, particularly the coloured kind,and – despite the knees-up action of some of these they now bring into the ring at the International – they liked a turn of speed. When I first went to London and found the pubs I joined a skittles team of whch the captain was a costermonger. He was an old sort himself and talked like Sam Weller without a letter V in his alphabet. If you made a good shot he used to say "Werry nice! Werry, werry nice!" He used to drive us to and from the away matches, all sitting in a row on his trolley. We had some exciting times over the tramlines in the rain with a cob that really could go.

On Sundays long ago the costers used to take their cobs down to Epping Forest for road racing and our skittles captain used to sing a London song that celebrated those races.

I remember the first lines:
>   'Down the road and away went Polly
>   With a step so jolly that she had to win'.

And the last:
>   'All the ones what come behind
>   They wished they never been born.
>   Woah Mare! Woah Mare! You've
>   earned your little bit of corn.'

8

Hunt Breakfast

When we were young we had no choice about fox-hunting. The people who bought the land within which we had our holding did so largely because they wanted to hunt across it. Since the whole district was in the hands of two houses at one of which the hounds were kept, and at the other of which they seemed to mass-produce daughters for marrying into the landed families, hunting was a big thing around our way.

The rich little girls started as toddlers on fat Shetland ponies, taken out by a retired groom on a leading-rein in order to learn the ropes. In old age they came out cackling and croaking on their side-saddles, dressed in black from head to foot and looking like thoroughbred witches. In between they were occasionally excused duty. When the season came round again and one of the young ladies failed to appear it was evident to all that she was in whelp.

Some of them rode with arrogant ferocity, leaping at any thing. Once her Old Ladyship parted from her horse in mid-air and landed in a big hawthorn bush. "Get me down, boy" she cawed, "Catch my horse, boy" – just like an old black rook in a tree.

But there were many who were timid at heart and this formed the basis of our very earliest commercial enterprise. On hunting days small boys were missing from farm work. They had taken up position for the opening of gates. Our knowledge of the countryside and the ways over which the foxes travelled enabled us to choose the best pitches.

Timing was important. The gate had to be opened just as the rider caught sight of it. Then it was possible to gallop on nonchalantly through, tossing down one of the six-pences that were kept in the palm of the left glove for the purpose. If the gate remained shut too long the rider would not risk being seen standing waiting at it. If others were coming on behind it might be necessary to risk jumping the fence and coming a purler. This was hard on the horse and thoroughly bad for business.

By the time we were seven or eight years old we boys had a good knowledge of hunting, and a better knowledge of the lie of the country and the habits of the local foxes than most of the people who rode to hounds. When I rode my own pony out over the land for the daily check on the beef stores, I could smell, as I opened a field gate, whether a dog fox had passed through the drain underneath. I lost that ability soon after I started smoking a pipe.

Although the tenant farmers had no choice about fox-hunting they would not have thought to question it. It was part of the pattern of life and in many ways we were tied to it. We were known to the hunting people of those days – even the Christian names of the children on the smaller farms. If people smashed through our fences the field master would take a note of it and a waggon-load of good fencing rails would be delivered.

It was a point of honour for members to buy their oats and horse-hay from farmers in their country. They got the very best, not only for the sake of our pride but because we knew the head grooms at the big stables would be exchanging comment on the quality that particular farmers had delivered.

The Old Man took a particular pride in his good horse-hay. Long before the days of modern ley-farming he planted one of our fields – Ram's Close – with a special seed-mix rich in vetches and clover. It was difficult hay to make, heavy and green and sappy at the time it was best cut. Either it wouldn't dry or left too long came down hard and woody. Mother said that it was no good talking to the Old Man when he was trying to decide whether to cut Ram's Close.

It is in respect of this that I best remember his contempt for the Anglican parson.

It was in 1922. The previous summer had been the worse drought ever and nothing grew. I took Tony up and down the field with the hayrake to gather up just two rows of bennets from where we used to carry waggon-loads.

Next Spring the opposite happened. Through weeks of warm rain the grass grew until the crop was enormous. Even with good luck it would have been nearly too big for the machines to handle. But the rains went on and on. We cut it in great rows when we could wait no longer and then turned and tedded it over and over again. Each time the rain came again. Late that autumn we tried to cart it off the field for the sake of the ground and the winter floods took the last of it off down the ditches.

It was on the day that we realised that we had lost the crop that I stood alongside the Old Man in the rain. We kicked the stuff that lay there like cold spinach and faced the fact that for two years running there would be no income from Ram's Close.

It was then that the Parson walked up from the gate beside us. Since we were friends of the Church even if not members, what would we be willing to give him for Harvest Thanksgiving? Eighteen years he'd had a country parish without learning to recognise the trouble we were in.

"I suppose" said the Old Man "you tell the ladies at your tea-parties that farmers are always grumbling about the weather."

That year the railways brought in hay for the hunting stables from other parts of the country.

The Hunts were also good about chicken. The farmyard fowls ranged free but didn't come to much harm – perhaps because the yard dogs kept an eye on them – but now and again you get a fox that takes seriously to poultry killing, especially a vixen with cubs. If you lost birds that way there was compensation to come from the Hunt Poultry Fund; that is, after they'd conducted a pretty strict investigation. And who can blame them? It was not unknown for the same dead birds to turn up on several smallholdings in turn. The old Hunt Secretary used to turn a blind eye. The younger one took to carrying the corpses away with him when he agreed to pay.

Still, they were generous and we thought it considerate, although we knew they had to ensure the farmers never got cross enough to start shooting foxes. A very strong taboo was maintained against doing that and, in that close society, you had to be a bloody-minded man to do it without agreement.

The Old Man would never shoot a fox although I have known him cause the disappearance of one if it took to raiding our poultry. As in all things concerned with country life he displayed experience and skill. He would find a tree close to the scene of the depredations that had a convenient branch seven or eight feet from the ground. Up in this, with a piece of string, he would tether an old hen. Down in the long grass below he would set a triangle of the old gin traps – now illegal. After dark the fox would come along his beat and scenting the hen above, jump to try and reach it. If he didn't drop in a trap first time he'd keep on jumping until he did.

Harry Hawkins once got agreement to shoot a fox and, like most things in his life, the incident ended in tears.

In some months of the year Harry left for the pub when it was still too light to shut the fowls up. On one such night he stumbled over to the henhouse on his return to shut them up. He didn't know that he had also shut up the fox who was already in there with them.

Next morning when he approached the henhouse there was no excited scuffle and, looking through the wire window, he saw the gorged fox sitting among a pile of dead hens.

In reply to his agitated complaint the Hunt Secretary said, "Well, if he's started that you'd better shoot him."

Harry got his gun. He instructed his boy that as he raised the pophole door the lad should rattle a stick on the back of the house. It worked. The fox bolted out, muzzle still flecked with white feathers, and made for the horizon. Harry squinted down the barrels, muttering encouragement to himself, and shot in the backside his horse that was grazing some way off.

It didn't do much harm. The vet had a jumpy half-hour probing the pellets out from under the skin, but the old horse never felt the same about guns. He was always very edgy if someone was shooting pigeons nearby. Harry stayed away from the pub for a day or two.

Apart from the poultry the Hunt had a Wire Fund. After the Great War the countryside was flooded with vast stocks of barbed-wire left over from Flanders. The fund provided payments to farmers who would ignore this economic aid and carry on with the ancient art of hedge-laying. A well-cut, well-laid hedge was a barrier to even an intrepid hunter. A shaky one reinforced with barbed wire could be a bloody catastrophe. So every winter we slogged away at hedge-laying. The job well-done is a thing of beauty and a very good barrier against stock. But it's a terrible lot of hard work.

When the hedge has grown up to shade too much ground and is starting to open up thin at the bottom then it is trimmed back and front. Then the tall sapling stalks are cut two thirds of the way through and laid down horizontally. At the same time they are woven in and out of stakes driven in eighteen inches apart and cut to the proper height of the hedge.

"How high?" I once asked the Old Man. "Cock high" he said. "Whose cock?" I said, and got my ears boxed.

The top was bound with twisted 'headers'. Next spring the sap flows along through the remaining bark of the laid branches and growth starts upwards from every bud. Thus the hedge gets a new start of thick growth coming right from the bottom.

The headers were usually of split hazel but old Jim Hynes, who won the hedge-cutting competition almost every year, used to go round in late summer cutting all the long, snaky briars that had grown out from the hedges. Rubbing the thorns off them he coiled them in circles and put them in a barrel of brine.

On the day of the competition he would get them out and say "Look now, young Jack, they'll tie like leather laces." That was his day. He always wore his billy-cock hat for it, though it went strangely with the ex-army puttees that were everywhere in the fields in those days.

So in six or seven winters we would work our way right round the farm. The boys had to do a chain each as soon as they were old enough. It was the best of all field barriers, proof against cattle and sheep. "Never mind sheep" old Jim would say, "you'll never see a hare get through mine."

But barbed wire is cheap and saves a lot of labour so in the end it pretty well obliterated the old art. But the Wire Fund delayed the change for a bit.

It was through the Hunt that we got our closest glimpse of the exorbitant luxury in the lives of those who didn't clean their own boots. For one thing they seemed to have an awful lot of people looking after them. There were then no horse-boxes and the hunters had to be hacked over sometimes many miles to the Meet. A groom called the second horseman had got up in the small hours in order that he could bring them over gently. In those days the very important were just taking to motor-cars and His Lordship would arrive in a large De Dion Boutan with as much polished brass as a stage-coach, driven by a chauffeur and accompanied by a valet with a big cane basket and any number of bottles.

He advanced to accept his first stirrup-cup in boots, coat and top hat that were magnificent. You couldn't see his breeches, which were of the finest powdered white buckskin, because he wore an apron over them until the very last minute. When the time came to move he instructed the second horseman as to where he would need a change of mount, handed over his apron and swung a leg over his horse in a cloud of white pipe-clay.

Twenty minutes later, of course, he was spattered with mud from head to foot.

Hunting provided the well-to-do English with a perfect opportunity to indulge their deep love of convention and ritual behaviour. Clothes had to be exactly right according to certain customs. Long coats or short coats, black or red coats (I never heard the word 'pink'), Bowler hats – which were invented for hunting – or top hats. The velvet riding-cap, now to be seen even on royalty, belonged only to the

Hunt staff. It was called a huntsman's cap and was worn only by them, with one exception. It was also worn by the farmers – not in black but in dove-grey.

All the farmers over whose land the pack hunted were entitled to ride with it. The grey cap was their badge, worn with market-coat and clean leggings. They rode their cobs, of course, and couldn't stay with classy horses on a fast run. But their knowledge of the ground and of foxes often allowed them to be there ahead of people who had galloped a lot further.

It was a different matter when one of the big half-bred hunters was ready for sale. Then one of the young farmers – usually big Bill Morris – would take it out and gallop unashamedly in front, splashing mud all day in the face of a selected gentleman who was rumoured to be looking for a young hunter. It usually worked. By the time Bill was home again and wiping his tack a groom would ride up: "The Colonel says to ask how much for the horse?"

Years later I was being interviewed to become a Tank Officer by a charming Colonel who, being too old for the fray, had been given the job of selecting the younger element. After a number of ordinary questions he suddenly said "Have you ever hunted?" "Yes, Sir." "Oh, really, which pack?" I told him. "Good", he said. Having been raised to straightforwardness I took a deep breath and added the words, "In a farmer's cap, Sir." "Excellent", he said, and gave a friendly smile.

For some minutes he asked me questions about it. I knew he was listening for turns of phrase that would give evidence of tribal membership. It was alright, I'd heard the language from childhood.

I knew that the Master was never spoken of as such but only just as Master. "Take your cap off to Master, boy." I knew that hounds never got the definite article. It was "Hounds are meeting tomorrow" or "Which way did hounds go?" That is a fairly subtle shibboleth. Anyone who has ever seen a blade of grass knows that hounds are not dogs. That's as bad as calling gun-dogs, shooting-dogs. I knew what it was to 'draw' and to 'lift', and that what is spelled like hulloo is called a holler. I knew when the warbling hunting horn said 'Going Home'.

In an equally English way there was room among the tight conventions of the hunting-field for some remarkable eccentricities. Old General Higgins, who had ridden with the cavalry over the African Veldt and been wounded in an unspeakably intimate way, was told by the doctors that he must never put a leg over a horse again. He went straight out and bought a lady's sidesaddle. To the wonder of all he hunted with his knee over the crook of it and his bottom bumping up and down until nearly the age of eighty.

It has to be admitted that hunting was one of the things that held the rural community together, enclosing rich and poor in a feeling akin perhaps to a Scottish clan. We knew nothing of what is now called class – class, I think, must be an urban institution – but there was a strong sense of 'station'. "God bless the Squire and his relations and keep us in our proper stations."

I remember a fox hard-pressed by hounds and his galloping Lordship, who disappeared down a rabbit-burrow in the corner of our Picket Field. Leaping from his horse the great man stared at the hole and shouted "Where's the bloody earth-stopper?"

"I'm here" said Jim Hynes, who was attending a gate nearby. For a pittance he had the duty of stopping fox-earths in our neighbourhood when the Hunt was due.

"Then why isn't this f .... earth stopped?"

"Because it'ent a bloody earth. It's a rabbit 'ole."

"Then why has the .... fox gone down it?"

"No s .... fox but one with you after it would have tried."

I listened with childish delight as the coronetted millionaire and the man who lived two weeks from the workhouse swore each other up in heaps. Every man stood tall in his station.

When the hunt met at our farm we used to have three millionaires to breakfast in the kitchen. They liked Mother's home-cured ham. One of them gave me my first saddle.

This was fox-hunting in its prime. To understand what has happened to it since it is worth taking a look at its history.

The history is unexpectedly short. Through Norman, Plantaganet, Tudor and Stuart times the beasts of the chase were the deer, the hare and the boar. To hunt them was then the privilege of gentlemen. For anyone else to kill them was poaching and followed by dire penalties. There were stag-hounds and buckhounds, harriers and, earlier, boar hounds. There were no fox hounds.

The fox was not included among the 'game' animals. It was 'vermin' and of no interest to the gentry. The beasts of the chase were also the beasts of the feast and no-one wanted to chew on an inedible carnivore.

These old times began to fade out when we turned from estate management to empire-building, when riches came less from rents than from the exploitation of colonies, when the industrial revolution began to move.

It was when this new world had established itself and the new people moved into big houses that the fox suddenly found himself the focus of attention. This new hunting was, in fact, a fashion, a trendy thing that swept through the 'yuppies' of the day. Adapting words of Whyte Melville one might say that now people hunted not for pleasure or provision but for the astonishment of others. The foxes, who for centuries had been threatened only by the snares of the peasants, provided the new people with excitement and a feeling that the noble prerogative of the chase had descended to them.

In 1780, at a Dorset country house, a man called Beckford, the scion of an adventuring banker family, started what may have been England's first pack of fox-hounds and wrote a book, *Notes on Hunting*, to set the others along the way.

In earliest days packs of hounds were made up of small groups that belonged to neighbouring huntsmen. It was the hounds who first had a 'meet'. When walking them across country to such a meet the huntsman would chain them together in pairs so that each acted as a check on the other and they moved along without running wild. That is why in the jargon of hunting there is still no such thing as a pack of thirty hounds – only one of fifteen couple.

Very quickly fox-hunting covered the country. The masters of Foxhounds (who used the honorific suffix MFH) divided the land into separate 'countries' and each hunted his own, except when he took hounds over to another by invitation. They came to use different parts of a country on different days. Monday country, Wednesday country. Then, as the well-to-do transferred from the land to the city, they came to have bye-days, usually at weekends, at which outsiders were welcome. On those days the Hunt servants collected contributions in their caps and a newcomer would tactfully enquire of others what the proper 'cap' was thought to be.

Each Hunt adopted its own style of dress – green, gold,

steel-grey and most often red – with variations in the colour of the collar.

Most important, each Hunt had its own style of buttons and these were to be worn only by invitation of the Master. Even a distinguished person moving from another district would have to hunt some seasons and put up a good showing before one day the Master said "Charles, I think it's time you wore the button." Proudly he would carry the silver buttons off to his tailor.

Nowadays you can get the precious button, and even the precious MFH, by writing a big cheque.

The changes started when the motor-car, and the horse-box, made it possible to hunt almost anywhere without needing a bed for the night.

It started in the earliest automobile days. Once the Hunt was meeting close to us for a bye-day and it seemed clear we might have them across our land. It was late in the season and the ewes were on the edge of lambing. Any harassment could be fatal. The Old Man told me to shut them in the rickyard which was surrounded by a big uncut hedge.

Later we heard the cry of hounds and saw with relief that they seemed to be taking a wide circle round the far edge of the farm. Then, much nearer, we saw a young horseman who was taking a line of his own to catch up. In top-hat and red coat he came bouncing down Lines' Hill. Without pause he drove his horse at the rickyard hedge and crashed through it to land among the heavy ewes.

The Old Man stormed out. Red in the face he shouted "You bloody young fool! You've no right to be out in the country! You wouldn't know a field of wheat from a field of blasted rickpegs!"

And then we saw it was the Prince of Wales and stood spell-bound.

For a long minute the future Duke of Windsor looked at the Old Man with tired eyes. He raised his top-hat and said, "You're a very rude old man, but I beg your pardon." Then he quietly rode away.

The Old Man was dreadfully shaken. He sat in his parlour chair, staring at the old photograph of the Yeomanry squadron, and never said a word all evening.

I wonder what he would have said about the present political controversy in which hunting finds itself. It is not over-burdened with reason or understanding. In his absence I will make a contribution. At least I know a thing or two.

I know that the fox can be a wild killer. I recently saw an announcement for a wildlife television programme in which it was said "Man is the only animal which kills more than he needs to eat." This is nonsense. The fox doesn't think about the housekeeping, he kills in response to simple stimuli. If something flutters within a certain distance of a fox he will kill it.

One night a gale blew a wooden window out of a turkey house in whcih we were wintering twenty-eight pedigree Marans. The fox, who like a policeman covers all of his beat every night, found his way in and killed all twenty-eight. As long as they fluttered he killed – and only took one away. The same thing happened to a neighbour of mine who specialises in Christmas geese. After digging under the wall of a corrugated barn the fox killed twenty-five out of a flock of one hundred. I expect the others huddled in a corner quietly, but every one that flapped was killed. A friend of ours last year put out thirty-six birds in a field-house, determined to produce genuine free-range eggs. A short time later they had eight.

I know that foxes almost always die instantly when hounds catch up with them, suffering less than they do from cyanide poisoning, inexpert shooting or game-keeper's snares.

I know that foxes are not particularly frightened by being hunted. Riding my pony as a boy I saw a fox come along and heard hounds behind. He sat down and took a rest. Scratched his chin. Walked round and picked a few blackberries. Then he cocked an ear towards the pack and trotted off in his own time.

I know that foxhunting may be a good sport but is a hopeless way of controlling foxes. Last year a fox was to be seen in our field every day of the week but the Hunt came twice without finding him. In the big vale below us hunting was stopped during the Great War because most of those who rode to the hounds were away in Flanders. The farmers were left to deal with things their own way and by 1918 there were no foxes in the Vale. A fresh stock was imported from Scotland to restart the hunting. Longer in the leg and lighter in colour than the ones we had always known. No wonder the hunting people who used to claim control now say that hunting is needed for the preservation of foxes.

These things I know. What I think is that despite the numbers of packs now hunting in Britain, fox-hunting will soon come to an end. I do not believe that it will be made illegal by a Labour Government. At the time of writing it looks unlikely that I shall ever see another of these.

Natural species die out not usually as a result of persecution but because of gradual changes in the environment where they used to survive. Such changes to the environment of hunting are well advanced.

The sport developed in the world of the great estates,

or in places where the land of a number of smaller squires was continuous. The break-up of those estates began after the First World War and has continued since. From my windows I look over the holdings of perhaps twenty different proprietors. Until 1961 all this land was within the estate of one old family.

Through changes in agriculture the farms have become increasingly unsuitable for hunting. Most of the corn when we were young was planted in the Spring. The horse ploughs could not have the land ready sooner. Now the plough and the seed-drill follow close after the combine and the land is full of winter corn. When the winter country was covered with stubble not much harm was done by galloping hooves. Now it's another matter.

The farmers are pretty good-natured. Some of them put notices on the gates saying "Hunt servants only." This is a polite way of saying that if hounds cross the land the huntsman may go with them, but we don't want the rest of you.

Even so, in the last two years, five farms I know have been forbidden to the Hunt. Fox-hunting won't stand a lot of this. One forbidden farm means that hounds must be held up all around it at a considerable distance if they are to be kept off it. Of course, a huntsman can risk it and apologise afterwards. But at least one court injunction has been granted that put hounds in contempt of court.

I must pay to belong to a shoot and stay within its bounds or I am poaching. I must pay to join a fishing syndicate and stay within its limits. It seems to me that for the fox-hunters, two hundred and fifty years of going exactly where they please has been quite a privilege.

There is another annoyance. In the old days when the hounds were heard a few yokels ran to the hedge to watch.

Today large numbers of people crowd the lanes in motor-cars. They are now called 'car followers' and the 'cap' is passed among them. It is really something to charge people for blocking a public road while looking over someone else's hedge at others enjoying themselves where they have a doubtful right to be.

As Byron said "I think the future is a serious matter." And now back to the past where I belong.

Great-grandmother in about 1880, a
dame of the West Riding clan.

Grandmother, about 1890.

Mother in 1901.

The Old Man.

Arthur Hargreaves, the Old Man, 1898, the mounted trail to the Paardeberg.

Me, 1942, the iron-clad road to the Rhine.

The three Hargreaves brothers. I'm on the left.

Off to College in 1929.

The farm. (*Above*) Six days of peace and quiet. (*Below*) The famous Shorthorns.

The farmer goes to market.

The farmer goes to his rest.

Quarterlock waggon. A year to build and a terror to drive.

Silvertail, the travelling artist's trotting champion.

The wanderer and the 'pukkering kosh'.

The huntsmen takes his hounds to meet in couples.

Off to flight pigeons with Cindy, the Kennet Valley cross.

First 'Out of Town' broadcast, 1959.   Last broadcast, 1981.

The only way to travel.

9
'A Shilling and a Pint'

I remember Queen Alexandra. She was still the leader of
fashion when I was little and I know two things about her.

First, she had an arthritic hip of the sort that would now
be replaced by plastic and consequently rode side-saddle
on the opposite side of the horse from usual. Recently I
saw an old wrong-sided side-saddle in a sale and wondered
if it might have belonged to her.

Secondly, she was the founder patron of dog-shows in
Britain and therefore must take her share of the blame for
the ruination of most of the dogs in the land. She may
have had particular responsibility for the sad fate that over-
took the Basset. When this fine hound was introduced
from France for hare-hunting – by the Heseltine family
among others – there took place the first of the many battles
that have been fought between those who work with dogs
and those who breed them for sale. It is said that the royal
influence was brought to bear on the side of the Show
Fancy – and the Basset was on its way to the Hush Puppy.

One may wonder how a dog as short in the leg as the
Basset could catch a hare. The answer is that with his
wonderful nose he followed the scent until he wore him
down relentlessly. A retired royal housemaid told the tale
of having watched a mouse proceeding down a landing at
the Palace followed a foot in the rear by one of the Queen's
Bassets who never looked up to see what he was pursuing.

Personally, I believe it should be made illegal to breed
and sell dogs commercially. Such an enactment would reduce

the number of dogs in the country by half – the right half.

In the old country dogs were bought for a purpose from men whose dogs could be watched pursuing that purpose. There was seldom a pedigree, which in any case certifies only that a dog has been born, but a great deal more was known about the significance of the breeding. Such evidence of lineage as did appear – as in the captions at the foot of old sporting prints – was likely to read "By Major Holding's Caesar out of Mr. Forbes' black bitch Melanie."

(I am constrained here to complain of a decay in English usage that has occurred since life moved from the country to cities. I heard a man say that he had two children by his wife. Impossible. It is *by* the male and *out of* the female. Children are born *by* Darren and *out of* Marlene. Or – in a superior strain – *by* Charles and *out of* Sarah.)

Our dogs were bred for a purpose, as originally all were. Some of them were local and were bred quite privately. There were strains of gundogs that were confined to particular estates and terriers whose home country was a single small valley. They were never passed around freely and certainly never thought of as products for sale. The Golden Retriever was first bred in a Scottish glen from a variety of ancestors including the bloodhound and a troop of yellow Russian performing dogs that the owner saw in a circus at Brighton. They leaked out slowly into the shooting world as now and again one was given to a favoured friend.

For a long time I wanted to get a puppy from an old man in our district whose terriers were unbeatable. At last when I knew there was a litter in his shed I broached the matter. He said he would think about it. I gave him time. A week later he stopped me and said "You can take a dog on if you want.""How much money?" I asked. "Money?" he muttered. "Well, give me a shilling and a pint."

Some of these strains gained wider fame. The best of the Hunt terriers were called Boddingtons, after their breeder Alf Boddington who was huntsman of the Whaddon Chase. People still boast of having Boddington blood in their dogs.

Major Edwardes at Sealyham in Pembrokeshire produced in twenty-five years – with tough working tests, selection and hard culling – a famous line of working terriers. One of his original dogs is stuffed in the National History Museum. It is difficult to associate it with the ones that were later shown under that name.

In this respect the oddest case is that of Parson Jack Russell. The evidence seems to be that he never bred a strain of terriers – though he did buy a lot. He was a raffish young man of the West Country squirearchy who was sent up to Cambridge to read for the Church. It took him three years longer than normal to get his degree in Divinity because he spent his time in the city's rat-pits. Every morning the Cambridge rat-catchers would deliver sacks of live rats on the competitive slaughter of which he and his companions would wager their dogs. He bought every dog that looked promising for the purpose – and chiefly the long legged, leaping terriers which were best at the game. Such dogs he would also need in the West Country when he returned home to become the famous hunting parson.

However, he was famed as a character and his name became associated with the sale of short-legged Home Counties terriers – very much closer to Alf Boddington's sort.

After the Second World War I was breeding a line of terriers descended from a Pytchley bitch and, having a litter for which there seemed no local vacancies, decided to advertise them in the local paper at thirty shillings.

"You're mad," said a friend from London. "Advertise them in *The Sunday Times* as Jack Russells and price them at fifteen pounds." The advertisement appeared on Friday, on Saturday they came in large cars – some of them with silver mascots of racehorses and labradors – and they bought the lot.

Such a market was not to be neglected. Inevitably soon afterwards the breeding fraternity started the battle to get the Jack Russell accepted by the Kennel Club in order that they could offer a branded article.

In Buckingham Palace there is a painting of one of the old parson's favourite dogs, presented to Her Majesty by a descendant. It's worth looking at.

For us, in the old days on the small farms, it was not so much a dog for a purpose as a dog for several purposes. For this reason we often had cross-breds.

For most of my childhood I lived with a wonderful dog called Tarzan. He was a first-cross Collie-Retriever. By this I mean not a Border-Lab. We never saw either of those. His parents were an English working collie, now extinct, and the old curley-coat retriever. He was a great all-rounder. He would drive the big bullocks fearlessly, hustling them and heeling them, yet he would bring sheep on very quietly. I used to go over eight miles to the railway yard to fetch a flock of lambs for us to grow on. I could bring them back across country when I was quite small, with the help of Tarzan. He would point a cock-pheasant that had strayed down our hedge, put it up and collect it if you shot it. He would sometimes leap with his front feet together on a tussock of grass and you'd find he was holding down a rabbit that he had winded. When we were ferreting he would find himself a place twenty yards down the ditch – just on the route the escaping rabbits would take – and chop them quietly as they came towards him. He would kill rats, chase cats and play ball with little children on the drying-ground.

We never bred from Tarzan. That is not to say that he had no children. When there was a bitch in season some-where – they say a dog can smell one three miles away – he would slip his chain and leave the straw-filled kennel under the barn. Halfway through the next day he would stumble home like a marathon runner just making the tape. If he did have any offspring they would be unlikely to be worth anything – unless he'd visited a collie or a retriever bitch.

There is something about the first-time cross-breds. It is a quality that breeders have always called 'Hybrid vigour' – a combination of the best of both parents. These individuals – which in plants are now called FI Hybrids – do not pass their virtues on if they are bred together.

Another cross-bred friend was Cindy.

As I grew and began to believe I was a great shooting man I was much affected by the talk of the knickerbockered experts in whose company I sometimes found myself, and I decided to save my money and get a Spaniel from a strain which was at that time thought to be the best. When I had just raised the wind and was about to splash out a farmer neighbour said to me, "Don't be a fool, boy! You're just buying words and newsprint. I'll sell you a better dog than that for thirty-bob." He took me up to the farmyard where his old Springer bitch was nursing a litter by the Head-keeper's Labrador. They were not exactly what I was thinking of.

He said, "They'll turn into better gundogs than you've ever seen at work." So – according to what the Old Man had always told me – I chose the smallest bitch. She looked like a shiny-black rather long-legged Spaniel and she turned out as he said.

Time and again I met other dogs of the same descent, all creditable performers. I learned that the farmers of Berkshire were particularly fond of them, and read in *The Field* magazine that there they called them the Kennet Valley Cross. After years of work with Cindy I decided, against all received opinion, to try and perpetuate her kind and mated her to a dog of the same cross, though not blood-related. She had sixteen puppies and the litter turned out – in the words of Freddie Threepwood – like 'a blasted zoo'.

Cindy and I, after years together through the woods and up the hedges, had full communication. Through a large vocabulary of words – and not only words but clicks and growls and hisses – I could tell her any number of things. That's how it is with dogs. The words don't matter – only the association. One man will say 'sit', and 'down', another will click his fingers, suck his teeth, stamp his heel. In each case the dog will sit if that is what he has learned.

A keeper once walked up to a shepherd on the hill who had at his heels a bob-tailed dog of suspiciously lanky proportions. "I don't think much of that brute," he said. "I'll bet it would snatch a hare." "A hare?" said the shepherd. "He wouldn't know what to do about a hare." As they walked on a hare got up and the shepherd gesticulated at it wildly, crying "Git On! Git On!" But the dog just sat down and watched it away.

As the keeper walked back and the shepherd passed over the hill another hare got up. "Sit", said the shepherd quietly, and the dog took off after it full-speed.

That dog, of course, was a lurcher. The lurcher is perhaps the most famous of the purpose-bred FI hybrids. It was always the dog of the poacher, the gypsy, the travelling packman and the rural miscreant. In partnership with such people the cleverness of lurchers was proverbial. A quiet old gentleman would walk on a Sunday morning apparently alone over the footpath through our place. In fact he had arrived on a bicycle accompanied by a lurcher. The bicycle was stashed in the hedge down by the gate and the dog had been sent off on its own. As he strolled along admiring the view of the hills the lurcher invisibly hunted the further hedges. When he got back to the bike the dog would be sitting beside it with three or four rabbits.

Another even more respectable senior citizen used to snatch the trout from His Lordship's stream with a noose of rabbit wire on the end of a beanpole. As he did so his small lurcher ran on sentry-go half a mile up the river each way, crossing the bridge to cover each bank alternately. Whenever anyone else hove in sight it would come back at full-speed. Parking his pole in the bushes the old man would sit on the bridge with the dog and smoke his pipe. "Good day", he would say, raising his bowler hat, and give him a while to pass on before getting out the pole again. Back the dog would go on duty.

Yet another man had a lurcher that would work a long net at night. This usually requires a team of three or four experienced beaters. The dog would do it alone, quartering the field like a pointer.

Nowadays the lurcher is fashionable. As a result of his rise to higher circles a number of misapprehensions have arisen concerning him. Lest the truth should die with me, I will elucidate the matter of lurchers.

From Georgian days onwards a favourite pastime among country gentlemen was field coursing – the hunting of a wild hare by a competitive pair of greyhounds each heavily backed by his owner. It was not like the coursing of today

– a spectator sport to which hares are imported – but took place between groups of friends across the open countryside.

The hounds by no means every time caught the hare and so they had to have means of judging the wager just on their running alone. They developed a set of conventions concerning the running in order that the Umpire, who galloped with them, could always declare the winner. One of these was that the hounds must follow precisely the course run by the hare, turning exactly with him as if he were towing the pair of them. Not a very good way of catching hares. Even though greyhounds are not very bright, in the end a dog would realise that by nipping across a corner he would cut off the hare. This was called 'lurching' and branded a dog as too clever by half. To avoid it they confined their coursing to first-season dogs that hadn't had time to learn. Thus, 'a lurcher' became a term of disapprobation among the Quality.

But not among the many. For the poorer, and more particularly for the mobile people of the countryside – drovers, shepherds, poachers and gypsies – a hare meant two good dinners. Their own working dogs were not fast enough, so they crossed them with greyhounds – what they called 'long-dogs' – particularly with long-dogs that were in disgrace for having learned some of the tricks of their trade.

So, in its second sense, 'lurcher' came to mean a dog that was a first-cross between a greyhound and a working dog, usually a collie, and particularly the 'Smithfield' collie that brought the beef-herds to London, or the old Blue Cattle Dog of the market drovers. Sometimes the cross might be a gun dog. In any case it had the hybrid vigour, a lot more brains and a sense of smell. The greyhound hunts by sight. Living all night and day with their masters, and travelling widely with them, these dogs became highly educated – unlike the greyhound that lived a kennel life between coursing days.

It is very difficult to breed an old-fashioned lurcher nowadays because the working-dogs in question are just about obsolete. At the shows that are held by the new lurcher fancier you will see a majority of dogs that are crossed greyhound – deerhound, greyhound – saluki and others. All these dogs are really the same dog in variegated forms. The family – jointly called the 'gaze-hounds' because of their sight-hunting – originated in the Middle East and is represented in the Egyptian tombs. As it spread it adapted. In the hot desert hunting gazelle the Saluki has a thin coat. Up in the further hills it grew an overcoat and becomes the Afghan. In Russian forests it developed a hard, protective coat and became the Wolfhound which in turn spread along Northern Europe to become the Deerhound.

All are gazehounds and to inter-mix them does not produce the FI hybrid virtues of a lurcher. They are just cross-bred long-dogs, produced originally for deer poaching but not much better at it I think than the greyhound itself.

There is one other long-dog hybrid that we knew very well long ago. It was bred between a whippet and a working terrier. Nowadays they show up classified as 'small lurchers'. We called them 'coney-dogs' in recognition of their profession. 'Rabbit' is, I believe, late Norman-French. The earlier English name for the creature was 'coney', so I expect these little dogs have been chasing them for a very long time. Many different terriers fathered them but if you could cross a whippet with the old northern Bedlington terrier you would get the very best.

I can trace only one man in England who still has the real old-fashioned Bedlingtons. You wouldn't want to breed from what are shown as Bedlingtons nowadays –

not unless you wanted a dog to skin and shove your nightie in.

Living full-time the lives of their masters the old country dogs were not only wise, but also quiet and obedient members of the family. Nowadays pubs in our district have notices saying 'No dogs allowed', and who blames them. Fifty years ago in the Five Elms on an evening there would be seven or eight dogs sitting quietly under the chairs of those who were playing cribbage and dominoes.

If a dog is to live a happy life with people he must be strictly civilized. The Old Man used to say that there ought to be no more than two kinds of dogs – good dogs and dead dogs.

A dog must be strictly civilized – just like a child. What have I said!

There is no need for cruelty – in fact a cruel man could never train a dog well. The thing is based on the fact that a dog in his natural state lives in a pack, a group of his own kind in which there is a strict order of precedence from the Top Dog to the bottom. This dogs regard as a normal state of affairs.

It was perfectly demonstrated for me once by the huntsman of the New Forest Hounds. The natural leader of that pack was an old Welsh hound called Medoc. He was really old and there were many young hounds in the pack who could have beaten him up if they had a mind to.

The pack was together in one of the yards and he sent me to open the gate. Then he put his horn to his lips to call them out. After a bit of musical chairs inside old Medoc trotted out of the gate. Then the rest followed after, no doubt in their order of precedence. Three times we did it, giving them time to get mixed-up in between. Each time the status of the Top Dog was similarly demonstrated.

So your home must be a pack of which you are the Top Dog, and you must start with the right puppy. In making that choice you must judge yourself because different people can do with different puppies. The shepherds used to talk of Hard Dogs and Soft Dogs. A hard dog is one that he is sure is the Top Dog and can be impossible to manage. A soft dog is nervous and against taking risks in front of authority. Some men said that if you could win the battle against a hard dog he would turn out best of all. Other people liked the one that was looking for instructions. Most people need a good middle dog.

It is best to see the whole litter, together with the bitch, and spend a long time watching them. You can observe how they relate to one another and how they react to you. You can clap your hands or suddenly bang down an iron bucket to discover which are frightened, which react with curiosity and which start barking furiously. In the end one of them will appeal to you as best. Usually the smallest bitch in the litter is a good one.

When training starts the attitude of the Top Dog serves as a model. When he wants to exert his authority he growls and a dog man has a low growling voice that he uses for instructions that must be obeyed. When he feels his authority is being flouted the Top Dog grabs the other dog by the scruff of the neck and shakes him. Dogs react submissively to this and shaking him by the scruff is just about the only kind of punishment ever needed.

In the old days I hardly ever saw a man hit a dog. For myself I only hit one once and that was for his own sake. A neighbour of ours started to keep geese and a terrier of mine, which was quite civilized with other poultry, decided these were something different and had to be attacked. Three times I managed to stop him before he'd done any real harm, but I knew that in the country a dog that killed other people's poultry would in the end have to be put down. The next time he went in I caught up with him and gave him a good hiding. I felt dreadfully guilty but he got the idea. But he always gave me a shifty look if he saw or heard a goose.

It seems a long time now since most dogs worked for a living. It's a shame because dogs really love work. My spaniel, lying asleep on the lawn in July, would leap up and dash into the study if someone just put the key into the lock of the gun-cupboard.

It took generations to breed into them the qualities needed for their job.

A couple wrote to me as a result of a broadcast. "We love your Bess," they said. "We have a labrador just like her but she never stops barking – all the time she barks." On enquiry it proved that they both went out to work and left the dog in a bungalow. "But we take her down to the post on the lead every morning." I told them I'd been on a hare-shoot on the Marlborough Downs. The farmer and I worked out we had walked fourteen miles. Bess certainly did five times as far – about seventy miles.

Our Master of Beagles told me that he had several times satisfied himself that his pack had done a hundred and fifty miles in a day.

Yet now, I think, some dogs are just fashion etceteras. In New York I watched a bell-hop take a brace of Afghan Hounds for a short walk in Central Park on the lead and then return them to the apartment block where they were confined. These dogs were bred to hunt beside galloping Arab ponies and would overtake an antelope.

As a child I only ever knew one man who owned a dog for the sake of looks. Henry Oakroyd was a very successful farmer who liked to give himself airs. He decided that in order to cut a dash he would buy a spotted Dalmatian Coach Dog to accompany him to market.

These dogs were descended from huge harlequin-marked guard-dogs that used to run alongside armed out-riders beside the coaches of the Balkan nobility as they drove through a countryside full of potentially rebellious peasants. As feudalism gave way to gentility they were converted to spotted dandies signifying elegance – pretty stupid but with a very charming nature.

Henry came into market with his Dalmatian trotting under the axle – a position they assume by instinct – and he caused quite a stir. Next week however it was noticed by an Airedale belonging to a butcher and it roared out of the shop after this offensive dandy.

Henry demanded that the dog should be shut up on Wednesday mornings but the butcher would not agree and the mayhem continued weekly.

However, Henry may have been silly but he was not stupid. He went over to one of the mining villages and borrowed a white bull-terrier. Having decorated it with spots of black enamel he tied it to the axle with a strong piece of string.

Out came the Airedale and found himself locked in combat with the fiercest fighter in the district. He quickly realised who was Top Dog and after that left the Dalmatian in peace.

file 148
page 103

10

Bang Goes a Penny

There are three reasons for going shooting. You can shoot for the pot, to destroy vermin, or for sport – and the latter is certainly the least justifiable.

Early on the boys became proficient at the first two, and later saw a good deal of the third in subsidiary roles though not often with guns in their hands.

The first weapon we ever handled was a little thing known as a No. 2 garden gun which was loaded with a tiny copper cartridge filled with just a pinch of dust-shot. I did hear that this was developed for the fruit-growers to protect the spring buds from the bullfinches, but for us it was part of the war against the rats.

In those days farms were infested with rats. The corn was harvested in sheaves and stored for a long time in ricks and barns. After threshing it was mixed and kibbled and fed loose from a sieve. Even the corn-bins were wooden and could be holed by the rats' teeth before you noticed it. There must have been a costable percentage of the whole yield that was taken by rats. And they pinched the fowls' eggs and would often kill baby chickens.

We would knock some corn out of a sheaf and leave it lying on the barn floor. After the rats had feasted there for a couple of nights we would get ourselves hidden in a gun emplacement of corn sheaves and lie there – still, silent and well smothered over – until the rats came out. Then – Crack! I don't know why we didn't start a fire. The fine art of that game was to get at least two and preferably three rats in line before pulling the trigger.

It was when we grew up enough to join the rabbiting brigade that we were first allowed to handle a real shotgun. It was not a very classy one – a 20 Bore with a heavy thirty-inch barrel, nose-heavy and straight in the stock. And, on account of our method of using it, it was just about the worst introduction to real shot-gun shooting.

To be allowed to use the 20 Bore was for us an initiation into manhood and, as initiations traditionally are, was accompanied by strict instructions.

We learned that a shotgun throws a charge of small lead shot that spreads wider and wider apart as it flies away. Close at hand the weight of shot is concentrated and its speed very fast, so that a rabbit shot at close quarters would be blown to bits. At a distance the velocity has dropped and the shot spread very wide, so that a rabbit shot at too long range would crawl away sadly damaged to die in his hole with festering wounds. A good shot fires only at the range – about 25 to 35 yards – at which the shotgun does its job decently. He must learn by experience to judge this range instantly.

The Old Man fired the gun first at an iron shed fifty yards away and showed us the ineffective scatter of shot. Then he fired it into a dunghill at a distance of seven feet. It blew a hole as big as a football in the solidly packed manure. Nowadays when criminals are shooting people up with sawn-off shotguns I think about that hole every time I read about it. As a result of what the Old Man did to our minds I couldn't now point a water-pistol at anybody. I get worried when I see what's in the window of modern toy-shops, because to point any kind of a gun at anybody was inexcusable.

He never allowed us to forget the dangerous thing we

had in our hands. Always know if its loaded. Never carry a loaded gun near anyone else. Carry it so it can be seen to be unloaded. Never put a loaded gun into a vehicle. Never bring one into the house. Never even bring one into the yard.

Once when I was coming into the yard with a rabbit he took the gun from me and opened it. It was loaded. I pleaded that I was just going to take the cartridge out but he slapped my ear and took the gun away for a fortnight. All boys in the country got this kind of discipline and it was worth it. In half-a-century of moving around with people using guns – millions of cartridges fired in all – I only once saw an accident; and that was when an American guest peppered a French one.

The reason why rabbiting was a bad start to shot-gun shooting was that we stalked the sitting rabbits, poked out the gun and held it still then pulled the trigger. This is what is disapprovingly known among classy shooting men as "taking a pot shot." As far as we were concerned they really were shots for the pot.

Shooting was not the best way to get rabbits. Those we carried to market to earn our pocket-money were taken with the purse nets or the long-net so that each was killed quickly and bloodlessly. These methods needed organisation and planning but when Mother said "Get me a couple of rabbits for dinner", there was no time to prepare an expedition. I would slip off with the 20-Bore to make a silent up-wind approach to where I knew rabbits were feeding. Creeping through a hedge-gap or crawling round a gate-post I would be ready by the time the rabbits were aware of me and sat straight up to look around. This way I could pick any rabbit and this way I learned to hold the muzzle up so they were never shot behind the shoulder. And this way, too, it was one cartridge per rabbit and that was all I was willing to pay for the family dinner because I had to buy my own.

I also had to deliver them oven-ready so I was a great rabbit-skinner while I was still in short trousers. Head off, feet off, turn the back-legs through and off with his jacket! Once when we took our sticks to beat on a classy shoot there were a lot of rabbits in the mixed bag. One of the guns put up a sovereign for a competition between the boys to skin three each. I won it. Mind you, I had helped the keeper select the rabbits for each of the boys.

Rabbits were an ancient pest of the farmlands – though perhaps not as ancient as we think since it is now alleged that the Normans may have brought them over. Indeed, there is no real mention of them until the Middle Ages and it may have taken until then for them to escape from their protective warrens and adapt to life in the wild. For me the trouble with this theory is that it seems to be accepted that the Romans brought the ferret. If the Romans didn't have rabbits what did they need the ferret for?

However, it was the rising multitudes of another pest that brought me to real shot-gun shooting. For twenty-five years of my younger life the countryside suffered a plague of wood pigeons.

I don't know why it happened. It seems that as the world continues to change different species of creatures in turn have their day. The vast herds of buffalo in America that were apparently only made possible when the prairie grazing had been suitably modified by millions of 'prairie dogs'. The very large numbers of Roe Deer in Britain today – probably more than ever there were in history – caused in part, I think, by the abandonment of the copses by the woodmen who used to work them all winter.

The Wood Pigeon – known in Shakespeare's time as the

Cushat – had always been around; but some changes in the climate of North West Europe or in English farming conditions resulted in the arrival at certain times of the year of flocks that could number up to five thousand. Hard weather brought them down from the breeding grounds in the North and when the corn was sown or was being cut, or when the winter green vegetables were being planted or were ready, they raided the countryside. Wood pigeons could double the price of Brussel sprouts at Covent Garden in a week. When War broke out and food became precious the Ministry of Agriculture gave away free cartridges for pigeon-shooting. Just my luck to be away at the time!

Now that great plague has passed away. Although the Wood Pigeon is still pest enough for its cost in human food to be calculated annually, we never see the great flocks that I remember. Times have changed again. Now the corn is off the field in a day instead of standing ten days in the stook. Now the stubbles with the spilled grain are ploughed within the week instead of standing for months.

I have no doubt that, leaving aside the few experts who accept the challenge of the zig-zagging snipe, wood-pigeon shooting is the highest form of the art of shotgun shooting. To justify such a statement the art must be examined.

The perfection of the shotgun was made possible by a Scottish parson. Up till the 1790s the charge in a gun had been ignited first by a slow burning match made of string and saltpetre, and later by striking a flint on steel. It occurred to the Reverend Foresythe that a little copper capsule filled with fulminate of mercury that went off crack when you gave it a sharp tap could be used to give an almost instant detonation. The Parson deserted his Ministry and came south to enter partnership with a gun-smith called Thomas Purdey who had been apprenticed to Mr Manton, the

King's gun-maker.

With guns fitted with the new caplock and a charge of shot calculated to form a circle of about 24 inches at thirty yards it became possible to shoot flying game in the air and ground game on the run. Apart from the incorporation of charge and detonator in a single cartridge that could be loaded from the rear, British shot-guns have been virtually unaltered since; and they are certainly the best in the world.

There remained one problem. The gun could not just be pointed at the bird which, during the time the shot was in the air, would have moved on. Indeed, it would move even further during the time that the message to pull the trigger went from brain to finger. Pot shots were no good. The gun had to move with the target and be kept moving.

There are some who try to guess where the bird will be at the crucial moment, pop the gun up and fire at the air where they think it will collide with the charge. The Americans call this "pointing out". It's a miracle if it works.

There are some who "give a lead". They swing in the same direction as the bird but a calculated distance in front. "How much lead are you giving them?" one man will call to another. "About eight foot." "Need a bit more I think. I'm sure I missed the last one behind." Everyone always does.

The best of them just swing with the bird and keep swinging smoothly, knowing that if the gun continues to travel exactly with the bird all calculations are unnecessary. In fact with the very best most of this seems to happen in the mind. It looks as if the gun just pops up and pots the bird, but if you watch the movements of the head, the neck, the shoulders, you realise that the swing has been going on from first sight of the bird and the gun is just added when it is needed. And you will see it follow through.

You look at the bird not the gun which has become part of you. It is more like a ball-game than shooting. In tennis you look at the ball and not at the racket. A good ball-player will quickly take to a shot-gun. It seems most difficult for a rifle shot – or a small boy who has been potting sitting rabbits.

Around the time the pigeons got started I had come into possession of a real gun. It was another gift from one of the hunting gentlemen – and absolutely the real thing. It was a Purdey. Long before it had been made by the best gun-maker in the world for some distinguished gentleman. (I realised much later that if I had asked them they would have looked up the old books and told me who he was. Every best gun carried a number.)

When it was made they had worked for weeks with little files on the hammers, the sears and the triggers until the action was sweet and perfect. He shot with it, no doubt, until hammerless guns arrived and then passed it to the Head Keeper. From him it went down the line until it reached some careless lower hand who had pitted the barrels by neglecting cleaning and then broke the toe and snapped the hand of the stock – no doubt by swiping at a wounded hare. Then it had been mended by an expert tinker with a bandage of thin copper sheeting. It had reached the point where it was suitable for handing on to a farmer's boy.

It was with this treasure that the Old Man instructed us in the art of shooting flying targets. His own gun was sacrosanct. "Imagine the bird has a sugar-lump balanced on his beak" he said. "Come up behind and swing through with him. Just as you knock the sugar-lump off his beak pull the trigger. And keep the gun going."

So, at last, to the pigeons. There were two ways in which the birds were tackled – at their feeding grounds or as they came to roost.

In wartime the Ministry encouraged and supported the 'flighting' at the roost. The birds came into the woods in the evening when many had finished work. The roosts were known so you could arrange for all those in a wide area to be manned on a particular day. But although the shooting was straightforward – all the birds coming at the same angle – the volunteers often fired at birds too high so that the whole area was filled with swirling high birds that wouldn't drop down until the light went. It was not often a success and cost a fortune in free cartridges.

The successful troops in the pigeon war were the hide shooters out on the feeding grounds. And boys, particularly out of school time, could find the hours needed for this.

Many of those hours were spent in reconnaissance, sitting in a high place with the Old Man's field glasses, working out where they would be feeding and how they would tackle the winds in flying there – then putting up the hide in the right place for tomorrow.

Still as a gravestone you sat in the hide with the gun across your knees. You turned your head slowly from side to side like a fighter pilot until you caught sight of a flock that might be pulled down to your dummy decoys. Then you froze.

If just one or two birds came they were left alone. They were the scouts and, if they found the place safe, then the rest would come swirling in from all sides. No game shooting provides so many different shots, so many different angles of swing to be calculated instantly.

Of course, you had to like being alone all day, except for the dog. Tarzan was perfect for the job. He was getting old now and had no instinct to rush about but would lie in the hide, emitting an occasional snore, until you roused him because one had dropped in a wood or the deep hedge or a high crop. Then he would waddle off and find it unfailingly. Through long hours of his company I became a 50 to 60 bird a day man, a pretty good performer. Micky, my tutor, once shot 250 in a day on a newly planted crop of field peas. They certainly knew how to find their food. I once saw an amazing concentration come from nowhere to a strip of radish seed that a local nurseryman had planted only that morning – so keen to have it that they took no notice of you.

Although pigeon control was applauded by agricultural policy it did not pay very well. There was a demand for them during food rationing but in ordinary times the price in the market could fall to eightpence a bird. The degree of skill required was such that a man who could kill two pigeons with five cartridges was considered a good operator. As a matter of fact I never got the marketing right until I started to leave the farm.

During my first week at college a sophisticated new acquaintance took me to supper at a French restaurant in Soho. On the menu it said "Demi-pigeon 4 shilling." "Are these wood pigeons?" I asked the proprietor. "Oui, Monsieur, English wood pigeon." It was a revelation. There was an eight hundred per cent mark-up between the decoy shot and the urban consumer.

Every week-end after that when I went back to the farm it was pigeon shooting. Each week I got back to my digs in London with the back seat of a second-hand bullnose Morris loaded. I did a barter deal that allowed me to take a friend to supper two evenings a week. And I didn't eat pigeon; I became familiar with the whole French menu.

Mother's pigeon pie was great. She knew the secret, which is that seven-tenths of the flesh weight of a wood-pigeon is in the two big flying muscles. There is no point in loading the pot with the bones of the little legs and the wings. In any case those are the parts that make the plucking of the bird most onerous. For Mother we just had pull off the breast feathers in two big handfulls and cut out the two big muscles with a sharp knife. The rest went in the bean trench for the benefit of next season's runners.

The flesh was marinated in olive oil and after light frying enclosed in the flaky pastry with chopped shallots and herbs. Delicious! And particularly good cold with a glass of cider.

So much for pests and so much for the pot. Shooting for sport was another matter. We learned about that because our services were often needed as part of the large organisation it involved.

In any case, in the two generations leading up to the Old Man's time shooting for sport in Britain had undergone a complete change for what many considered the worse.

When Mr Pickwick went shooting at Dingley Dell, the time of the great shooting prints, gentlemen went shooting in twos and threes usually outnumbered by their dogs whose work was their main delight. They walked miles in the day over rough ground wherever the noses of their dogs took them. The bag was mixed and small – still closely related to the home larder – and apart from what would be eaten by the family there would just be a brace or two for giving to friends.

Then 'driven game shooting' came to England. It was imported from the relatives of Prince Albert. In central Europe the Arch-dukes to whom Albert was related were accustomed to send out armies of peasants to form a circle round the countryside. For perhaps two days they would move forward slowly, driving every living thing slowly towards the Schloss.

There, on scythed grass, the grandees sat on chairs with their guns and admiring women-folk. Servants surrounded them – loaders, keepers, butlers. As the game grew close they stood to do execution. The size of the bag was evidence of skill, also a testimony to the grandeur of the estate.

In Britain this method was adopted chiefly for pheasant and partridge shooting and was in the beginning very unpopular. The estates developed a passion for privacy, enforced by new armies of gamekeepers. People were turned away by these fellows when walking along paths where their ancestors had always walked. One great expert, 'Stonehenge', the *nom-de-plûme* of an early shooting editor of *The Field* , referred to it as 'this odious continental battue' and mourned the fact that it was the end of real dog-work. The Old Man agreed with that. When he was young he used to tramp miles with a leash of trained spaniels. Now the retriever had replaced them – and the setters and pointers – and just had the job of fetching and carrying on demand. He called them 'wretched servants-hall dogs.' Of the guns who now stood in line at numbered pegs to which, if necessary, they could be conveyed on wheels, he said "They've taken no more exercise than a game of croquet."

It was a very expensive business. There was a saying about it – "Up goes a sovereign, bang goes a penny and down comes half a crown."

Some of the money came our way. The keepers wanted our tail corn to feed the pheasants; they came round in the spring to collect broody hens for their rearing fields: they let us into the home-shoot rabbiting as long as we left them enough to feed their retrievers and in the absence of actual peasants they needed large numbers of boys to come beating at two bob a day. By tapping our sticks through endless days of this we learned all about the game.

They did us a favour now and again but you had to watch them. The Old Man thought up one of his proverbs, which seemed later to apply to almost every sphere of life I've walked in – "If you have a hare from the keeper, you'll never finish paying for it."

Now driven game shooting is pretty well universal – all incubators and pellet-feeding. When myxamatosis took the rabbits, I.C.I. cartridge sales so plummetted they started a publicity campaign called 'Game is a crop.' Now one farm where four of us, three farmers and a doctor, used to dog it for forty pounds a year has a syndicate of twelve guns on it each paying £1,200 a year.

It is still dominated by the numbers game. "How many have we shot?" "How many did you shoot?" It's a macho affair, obviously a traumatic release of office tensions for the middle-aged well-to-do.

But you never see many old men in the shooting-field. I haven't fired my 12-Bore for five years, except once at a magpie that wouldn't leave a hen and chicks alone. I do know one fellow who still likes to blaze away at the age of eighty, but then I always thought of him as a case of arrested development.

It happened to the Old Man much earlier – perhaps on account of the Boer War – so that we were only occasionally reminded what a fine shot he was. Once towards the end of winter when the wild duck were flighting around in twos and threes he decided we'd have a pair of them for dinner. He put a couple of cartridges in his pocket and when he walked round that evening he had his gun crooked open over the left arm. As we stood against a hedge a pair came flighting round. He waited ages to see they were going to circle close enough. At last – far too late it seemed to me – he took out the cartridges and loaded up without any hurry. He put the gun up quietly and killed them both in mid-air. They just changed shape in full flight and fell to the ground without a flutter.

Recently at a classy shoot I saw two top clay-pigeon shots hidden behind the line to finish off the cripples.

11

Cash Flow

It is odd that – considering their importance to our early
lives – I have hardly mentioned the cattle. The truth is that
since I grew up I have never ever wanted to have anything
more to do with dairy cattle. You can't even switch them
off on Sundays.

If sometimes I make the mistake of talking about the
past to the young people of today they interrupt me by
chorusing their defensive slogan, "I know! You had to
walk three miles to school!" As a matter of fact it was rather
more than three miles; and the matter was made worse
by the fact that before we set off for school we had to go
milking.

The way in which small farming people are inescapably
tied to the dairy cow is reflected more strongly by the
milk-lakes and butter mountains of modern Europe. A
corn-grower takes a year to turn over his money. The beef
producer waits twenty months for his, or in our day, with
the demand for more mature joints, three years. All our
breeds of sheep, except one, produce both their lamb crop
and their wool clip at twelve months' interval. Apples were
picked once a year, and once a year the geese were fattened.
Only the dairy cow and the laying hen produced something
saleable daily.

They were the cash-flow animals. They produced subsi-
dence and the weekly housekeeping money – while all big
spending waited for the annual returns.

The early social improvers said that to live a good life a

cottage family needed two acres and a cow. Even those
without land kept cows. On the open commons where
cottagers still exercised rights a bunch of them would be
grazing among the gorse bushes, each wearing a cow-bell
slung over its neck with an ash-crook and two leather
thongs. The bells were made by the blacksmith, hammered
out of sheet iron and rivetted together with an iron nut
hanging inside as a clapper. Each one had a different note,
according to iron offcuts he was using, and once the note
was familiar any particular cow could be located as it grazed
in the thicket.

Where there was no common-land a family would often
keep a roadside cow that fed its way down the verge like
a gipsy horse in a collar and chain. I know one old man
who, up a lonely lane where cars are scarce still keeps
such a cow – and still cuts his winter hay with a scythe
by the roadside. They always looked fit, the roadside cows,
just as the gypsy horses did. The rich mixture of herbs
gave better nourishment than any enclosed field. That is
how *Anthriscus Sylvestris* got the name Cow Parsley. I often
think of the millions of tons of animal feed that now fall
to the Council mowing machines – though increasingly
today you see that a goat-keeper is claiming the right.

Looking now from the highest hill over the dairy vale
below there are three differences to be seen that would
have made the place unrecognisable to the Old Man. The
Dutch beetle has killed all the elm trees and opened up
the view remarkably. The cornfields are no longer stained
red with poppies. And the land, as far as you can see, is
inhabited by black-and-white cows.

These Friesian cattle – sometimes called Holsteins if
they've been to Canada and back on their way here from
the Baltic fringe – were unknown in Britain when I was

born. The oldest line-bred herd I know was founded in 1921 and it was not until after the Second War that they replaced our old Shorthorns. When they did so the genocidal sweep was as complete as the obliteration of the Greek population in Asia Minor.

When they now make films of Thomas Hardy's stories and take great trouble to get the historical detail correct, they nevertheless still have black-and-white cattle. I don't suppose they could find the Shorthorns, even if there were someone who knew to tell them they should. Certainly none of Hardy's characters ever saw a Friesian.

Our old Shorthorns were roan and white – sometimes red or blue and white – and their horns which they wore every day of their lives twined neatly forwards, unlike the flamboyant Longhorns which had left two generations earlier for the American west. They were dual-purpose cattle breeding both heavy milkers and the big beef bullocks, just as the red Sussex cow used to produce everything from milk to the great oxen that pulled the wooden ploughs.

The number of dairy cows on the small farms was usually 12 to 14. We thought we were big people because on average we had just over forty cows in milk. Now a good man was reckoned to milk eight cows an hour by hand, so we had to put in more than ten man hours a day of milking before any other work on the farm got done. Also it was held that cows were healthier and milk-yield maximised if the interval between milkings was even. So it was six in the morning before school and six in the evening before tea and homework. Three hundred and sixty-five days a year. It's difficult to go on loving them.

In mid-winter both milkings would be done in the dark with just a single hurricane lamp hanging inside the door.

As a matter of fact this provided an excellent opportunity for learning about life. The two men milking side by side would forget the lad sitting quietly down at the dark end of the byre and proceed to the discussion of things that were not normally mentioned in our presence.

I wonder if I could still milk? I am sure that if you handed me a three-legged stool my left hand would swing it round behind my bottom; and I suppose that the pattern of muscular movements so difficult to learn is still somewhere in my memory store. For milking, whatever gesturing comics may think, is not just a matter of pulling up and down. That is the way not to milk. The sight of passing cows with long pendant teats revealed to us that they belonged to a bad milker.

The job is done by a squeezing motion of the fingers in succession that produces a rolling pressure – in technical terms, an artificial peristalsis – that reproduces the motion of the suckling calf's tongue. It is very tiring until your muscles have been long hardened to it. In the War when we learned revolver shooting they gave us a long series of hard finger exercises that produced just the same ache in the forearms.

When the job is well done the rhythmic overlapping of the motion of the two hands produces an almost continuous low roar of milk entering the pail. It's sad that a knack so hard to learn should now be so useless. The modern dairy-man, in his mechanised parlour, handles 150 cows himself. And you might have to go through several dozen farmers to find a skilled hand-milker.

All the cows in our herd milked pretty quietly. For one thing they had known us since they were born because the herd was entirely home-bred. Every year nine or ten young heifers calved for the first time and came into the dairy, and each year ten cows went to market as fifth-calvers. That was when they were worth the top price. It was one of the Old Man's principles never to keep on the place anything that was declining in value. "Except me" he said. "You won't get rid of me until I'm ready."

It was thus that every year the yield of the herd had been improved. It rose by an average of more than a gallon a day per cow during my childhood years. And that was before we had scientific knowledge of dairy-feeding, though the body of it was forming and was soon to come to us.

Every four years or so he would change bulls, in order that they were not used overmuch on their own direct descendants, and when he did he would try to get a bull from Mr Downfield's 'Wildeyes' strain. 'Wildeyes' had been a famous cow in earlier days when farmers were perfecting the Shorthorn and her name was still known to everyone.

The trouble was that the Wildeyes bulls tended to be a bit chancy. The fact is that all bulls are chancy. Once they get three years old and upwards they are very dangerous animals, even more so because their outbreaks of violence tend to come intermittently between long spells of placid behaviour. A man really used to cattle will never take a risk with a bull and regards as a fool anyone who would.

A bull more than six months old had by law to have a copper ring in his nose before he could be taken on a public highway. With a lead-chain attached to this he could usually be managed if it was done sensibly. Often instead of a chain a bull-stick was used – a long pole with a clip on the end. With this his head could not only be pulled towards you but also held away. Even so the strength of a bull when he is angry can hardly be imagined. Once in the

Market I saw a young Jersey bull – the smallest breed – that had lost his temper. There were four men on the bull-stick trying to control him but, despite the pain to his nose, he shook his head and flung them all against a wall.

The most frightened I ever was – apart from the War when, as soldiers know, all soldiers are always frightened – was when a bull of ours got loose with his chain dangling and wandered off to stand in the shade of a loaded haycart that had been left propped up on a rather shaky trestle. Through shaking his head on account of the flies he had caught the chain on the tug-hook of the shaft.

As I approached him he did it again and the load shook like a jelly. The Old Man was out, my elder brother was away getting educated and I had to get him unhooked.

So bulls are no joke. Except that old Jim Hynes, whose sense of humour was very questionable, had a joke about them. One day when two hikers were looking doubtfully over the gate of a field where a bull was, he approached them with the aim of giving useful advice and said, "They'm alright – if you knows how to handle them. If he comes for you just grab him by the balls. He can't do nothing then." He cackled his way off and left them wondering if he meant it.

Of course, a lot of the trouble came from the way most bulls were kept on small farms. For safety's sake they were kept in small strengthened boxes. They were let out in the yard to a cow that needed them and when it was over fed back into the box. Their diet was unpalatable. On smaller farms the hay that got spoiled by the weather was piled up in a little round stack called the Bull's cock (as in 'Haycock' you understand). They were rarely exercised.

Nowadays the best bulls never see a cow and there are cow-men who never see a bull. Artificial insemination has

taken over for dairy breeding and such bulls as are seen
in fields are beef-bulls who do an outdoor job on the de-
selected cows. You will have noticed that you most often
see black-and-white cattle with a red-and-white bull.

Not long after I became a student we had a lecture from
a research professor who told us of the things that were
being learned about insemination, and the stranger things
that would follow it. The implantation of ova, for instance,
that might one day allow a top cow to have ten calves a
year instead of one by use of other host cows. "Does this
mean" I asked, "that a woman wil be able to let another
woman have her children while she does a job?" He found
the question distasteful. "Obviously" he said coldly "such
things as these will never enter into the human sphere."
I wish I'd had a bet with him.

Nowadays, of course, the very best bulls are available
to everybody and their breeding value is assessed by progeny-
testing their offspring. In the old days impregnation seems
to have been thought of as just a mechanical process – like
turning a switch – and the breeding, as with Arab ponies,
was through the female line. Perhaps that is why names
like Wildeyes are remembered.

The Old Man's breeding decisions were taken on Sundays.
Every Sunday afternoon he gazed at the cows. He would
sit on the gate and look at them for two hours on end. Then
he would get down, knock out his pipe and say "Ay!" In
that time he had been through every generation of every
cow. He had run through their relationships to one another
and gone through all their milk yields. He would check
through what he had been able to discover about the after-
sales performance of some he thought he shouldn't have
parted with. Each week he revised his ideas of whose
calves he wanted to enter the herd in three years time.

I only once remember him neglecting this ritual and that was on the day after he'd been struck by one of those sudden blows that often used to come to farmers – and sometimes still do.

It was during my first vacation home from college. As I walked round the place with him to catch up on all that had happened in term-time the farm for the first time seemed very quiet. I had come from my new digs in a London High Street where the pubs turned out at night to the sound of singing and fighting, the flares danced over the street-sellers' barrows and the Bedford Music Hall had been featuring a young comic singer from Lancashire called Gracie Fields.

We turned through the gate of the Close to inspect the pride of the farm, the ten young down-calving heifers just due to come into the dairy. Six of them were dead.

Fit, fat and unharmed, they lay stone dead on the ground. They had fallen where they grazed and the last four still grazed around them.

I felt tears as I looked at his stony face and thought of how for years he had sat on the gate and planned the breeding lines that had brought them to perfection.

At last he said, "It must be the Bedfordshire." For several months the farming papers had been reporting these sudden deaths and calling them Bedfordshire Disease after the place where they first occurred. "And your lot can do nothing about it!" After only one term he'd got me classified among the scientists. "And no more can God Almighty!" I'd always suspected he had his doubts about him.

Now, of course, something can be done about it. It was a deficiency condition, known today as Hypo Magnesia, that can be cured and, indeed simply prevented. The same is true of Milk Fever, known to us just as 'Going Down' which struck cows just as they first came down with their milk.

These troubles came upon us unexpectedly because they were the results of success. For a century, from the time of the great agricultural improvers to when people like the Old Man worked full-time to improve their production, their results were ahead of the knowledge of animal nutrition.

But the willingness to take advantage of new knowledge is characteristic of farmers, far more so than in the case of many industrialists who might think of them as hayseeds. After the 'Bedfordshire' the Old Man really went in for minerals. On every gatepost were the zinc clips that held the blocks of minerals balanced to particular prescriptions. "What are they?" said a visitor from the town. The Old Man assumed a professional pose with his thumbs hooked under his lapels. "In the wild state" he said "cattle migrate thousands of miles in search of the minerals that they require. Now you will readily perceive that my cows can't bugger off to Droitwich." Droitwich was the only spa he'd ever heard of.

In the Old Man's young manhood and in my infancy, animal health was a medieval business – almost a matter of witchcraft – with little knowledge of causes and not much idea of protection. Veterinary work was pretty backward, though on the brink of a great move forward, and in any case rather than face vet's fees the small farmers preferred to rely on local wise men. One of those in our district was old Mr Ayres. He recommended that for 'Going Down' a frog should be burned in the gateway through which the cows came in to milk. I think not much in the way of minerals is liberated by the burning of a frog.

For a small man with a pride in his herd the continuing anxiety was what we knew as 'Jones Disease'. It was a violent dysentery that racked a cow away to nothing in no time. We called it 'going screw'. Even so the only thing done when the symptoms first showed was to pack the 'screw' off to market while it still had enough flesh to be saleable. This meant that it travelled on foot with the drove down the green roads along which everyone's stock went to and from the market – and squitted its way along every yard of it. Today, of course, there are cattle-waggons and very strict rules for keeping markets free of disease.

Knowledge was moving forward though, and the first research scientists were beginning to travel the country and talk to the farmers in the field. They were a very odd lot.

At first sight Sir George Stapleton was astounding. He was the man who developed ley-farming and he came to explain to the men on the land that grass was a crop to be managed and not just a gift of nature. His monocle glinted under the brim of a straw-boater. He wore bow-tie, college blazer, white cricketing trousers and spats. He hopped about waving a gold-knobbed malacca cane. His gestures were as extravagant as today's television botanist. Perhaps they're all the same?

Quite unlike him was the blunt Dr Robert Bouflour who worked out the principles for the feeding of dairy cows according to yield. He was available to farmers everywhere, becoming known and loved as 'Bobby Boflower'. He had a north-country accent and was distinguished for his directness of speech. Once, when he was lecturing in our village-hall, one of our more backward neighbours rose to ask a question. "Tell me, Doctor. I got a field lays down along the brook and tis always wet. Them rushes grows there and chokes up the grass. Can you tell me what to plant in it?" The answer is well-remembered – "Drainpipes, you bloody fool!"

Although I left the veterinary road long ago I am proud
of the huge advances that have been made in this field.
They could only have come about through the complete
co-operation between the technicians and people like the
Old Man, conservative at first sight but devoted to the
craft of agriculture.

It was this combination that laid the ghost of perhaps
the most insidious evil that used to haunt dairying – Bovine
Tuberculosis.

There is no doubt that when I was young the milk was
well infested with this bacillus. Dairying was very dirty
compared to nowadays and all a small farmer thought he
needed do about hygiene was to white-wash the inside of
the byre afresh each year.

It was alright in the countryside. The milk was distributed
so quickly. It went to butter and to cheese. It was put in
the churn as soon as it was cooled and taken off on a local
milk-round. But when the railways were complete and the
cities grew fast the milk began to travel hundreds of miles
and to suffer slow mass-distribution. The TB bacilli were
given time for their galloping growth. By the time I was
running healthily across the grass there were hundreds of
thousands of children in the cities whose glands were swollen
with Bovine Tuberculosis. Earlier, you see, when the aggre-
gations were smaller, their milk would have come from
cows kept within the city limits. I'm told that Liverpool
still had city cow-keepers until well after the First War.
Probably a good thing.

Once the nation was aroused to this there took place a
remarkable cooperation between bureaucracy and free-will
by which every cow in the country was tested for tuberculosis. As a result of it Britain became the first country
in the world free of Bovine Tuberculosis.

I saw this happen and took part in it. As a young assistant at the local practice I experienced all the bucolic comedy of the Veterinary Life. I sometimes think James Herriott must have shared my dreams.

But then came the T.T. testing. At the rate of at least one herd a day we lifted the tails of cows and injected them, returning a few days later to measure the size of swellings between two silver balls on the end of a special pair of callipers. It seemed to go on for ever. After manipulating the teats of cows through most of my childhood I had moved upwards just two feet to the sub-caudal fold. I began then to feel that I was chained for the rest of my life to a dairy-cow's backside.

12
Yesterday's Men

During the Age of the Shorthorn – after the Longhorns crossed the Atlantic and before the Black-and-White cattle crossed the Channel – the people were very skilful. The evidence of the tasks they performed is to be seen hanging on the walls of pubs all over England. These artefacts were first exchanged for half-pints by the old men of the period during their last days when they hobbled around the village on two sticks. They had become redundant in an industrial change that got rid of a quarter-of-a-million farm hands without anyone seeming to notice. Had they been miners or social-workers we would have heard about it.

The evidence of the tools that are now displayed is often misinterpreted. Most of them are quite local and many of them very specialised, so that it is a bold man who sets up to be an expert on them. Even the yokel's tool-of-all-work, the billhook, exists in dozens of different shapes and sizes.

An old friend of ours who ran the threshing engine went to the blacksmith when he was a young man and got him to make a little sickle-hook – hardly bigger than a cut-throat razor – which he used all his life to cut the bond on the sheaves as he opened them up and slid them onto the canvases of the thresher. It was perfect for this task for which, generally, people favoured a lino knife.

When the threshing-machine finally packed up we made a film to record how it did its job and showed the little hook. An expert wrote to tell me that I was quite wrong about the use of it. "Such hooks," he said "were invariably made for the harvesting of tick beans." This one wasn't. We never saw any tick-beans. An uncle of mine used to grow a few but he lived over where he could sell them to the pigeon-fanciers.

Some of these tools are so specialised that they may never be identified. There were quite a few in my collection when I gave it to the local museum that no-one could put a purpose to. As a matter of fact, we have just discovered the truth about one after five years of trying. It is a very large combined mattock and drag with a hole that takes a thick, and therefore probably rather short handle. The blade on one side is broad and heavy. The two tines are sharp and fourteen inches long.

The most popular suggestion was that it was for planting and subsequently earthing up potatoes. I've grown enough potatoes to know that it would be hopeless for that. At last I found an old man who knew it, in fact thought that it once might have been his. There never were many about, he said.

In the chalk country the old houses were built of the great flints which, year by year, rise up through the chalk. Under the influence of the plough, perhaps, they come up to show at the surface but don't break free. At the time of the stubble, and when the sheep were in hurdles on the chalkland, this old fellow went out with a horse and cart to collect the flints for building. As soon as he demonstrated how he dug away round the flint and then levered it out of its seat the clumsy thing could be seen to be perfect for the task. Now the label says 'Flint Pick'.

Even if the purpose is obvious you would be unwise to make even a rough guess at the age. I have a shepherd's crook that was found when ditching on a property called

Shapwick, which is what a sheep farm was called in Saxon times. It is an elegant piece of smith's work but almost exactly like the one made in the forge for the father of our local shepherd. How far apart were they made? Five hundred years? Only a metallurgist could tell.

The village blacksmiths made the pikes for the Peasants' Revolt and some of them even made them again in 1940 for Dad's Army. In between they made everything that anybody did anything with, and so the forge had always been the centre of the village. It was the place where news was exchanged and where small boys kept warm on a winter's day and learned something about everything.

A man would come in with a curly ashpole cut from the hedge a year earlier because it would just make a sned for his scythe. Now they had to be fitted together and it was long job to satisfy him. Ten times the blade would go back to the fire for the heel of it to be turned or twisted a fraction. Each time you heard the rurping breath of the bellows. Then the hiss of steam as the iron was quenched and refitted for another try. "Turn her heel up a bit, John. Point's low." "Have to go over a mite, John. Edge is looking down." In the end as the old fellow swayed it across the floor the blade would travel flat and parallel a quarter-inch off the ground – ready to take a long, slicing cut of the grass instead of chopping at it.

That done, the blacksmith would turn to the next of a thousand jobs. He was endlessly patient and always good-natured. I think that blacksmiths, with their strength and social importance never had anything to prove, like heavyweight boxers who never get into a fight outside the ring – except of course if they've had a losing run.

If the next job was with heavy iron then soon we could hear the famous rhythmic ring of his sledge bouncing between the work and the anvil – the sound that could be heard further across the landscape than the church bells. "Kerlanker! Kerlanker!" A traveller out of sight of houses could tell that a village was ahead of him.

As the sound travelled further it lost its lower frequencies more and more and rose in pitch until it became just a tinkling version of itself. If you listen to the call of the Great Tit you will know why we knew it as the Anvil Bird. "Klinker! Klinker!" it goes – a tiny anvil far away.

On the other side of the street Harry Brandon would have been glad to see the mower go on his way and heard the heavy hammer start to ring. He was waiting for John to weld up the heavy iron lock-rings for a waggon that was coming to completion.

Harry was the wheelwright. It might have been truer to call him a wainwright since in the village his trade was heavy waggons and carts for the farmers. The traps and gigs and floats and ladies' chaises were made by the bigger firms in the market-towns, drawing their trade from all around. But since the wheel was first invented the men who built vehicles have been named for it, because it was the wheel that made them possible. Given the wheels, any reasonable woodworker could make some sort of a job of the rest. And, no doubt, did. In one district close by a cart was called a 'pair of trucks'. 'Truck' is just an old word for wheel. A truckle bed is a bed with wheels made to be pushed under another one.

So Harry was a wheelwright. He built the first waggon the Old Man ever had, just about when the Old Queen died. They ordered it after one harvest to be delivered in time for the next. Mother told me that they paid half in advance and saved all year to have the balance ready. It was forty pounds altogether.

Harry would build a waggon only as he thought it should be. Nobody argued because there were several in the district still in work that had been built by the Brandons a hundred years before. You could recognise them; but then once you knew the area you could recognise where each waggon or cart came from. In each place where they were made there was a family of wheelwrights who long ago had agreed with the local farmers what waggon was needed for the slopes and the soil and the roads and the crops of that district. Thus in the museums now you will see Sussex Waggons, Berkshire Waggons, Hereford, Dorset and Norfolk Waggons.

For generations it had been a point of pride with the Brandons that none of them ever used any timber he had bought himself. That was put down to season for his son while he drew on the stocks that came from his father. In the big open hovel behind the shop Harry had a marvellous stock to draw upon, such timber as has not been seen since the two wars. Harry maintained the tradition. He bought ash for shafts and elm for body planks, bent oak boughs selected on site that would cut exactly to make the knees; and, strictest of Brandon rules, apple for the naves, which is what he called hubs. Most officianadi of rural tradition will tell you that the naves were made of elm, but whenever a big apple was being cut down in the district Harry had to be told. He cut it up into nave-blocks and put it away for his son, never knowing then that his boy would be welding up steel tractor-trailers.

When I was little there was no single power-tool in the shop. I used to go there to watch the men working in the sawpit. At the end of the shop, flanked by a shutter window each side that could direct the wind for blowing the sawdust, was a pit just about the size of a human grave. Above a big trestle with a top made of two planks with a gap between, through which the saw could pass. Between them were beams on which the wood could be laid.

The top man stood on the trestle and pulled up. The pitman stood in the hole and pulled down. (Now you see why engineers call the bearing at the bottom of a crank-shaft the 'Pitman bearing'). Between them they worked the long two-man saw. The pitman's job was the one to avoid. He couldn't even look up to see how things were going without getting his eyes full of sawdust. The topman holds the line.

Sometimes we can see an old pit-saw in a sale, and usually hear somebody say, "Look, there's an old cross-cut." That is exactly what it is not. A cross-cut saw works across the grain. A rip-saw works along the length of the wood. The teeth are filed quite differently. Pit-saws are always rippers. The saw-pit fell into disuse because Harry lashed out and bought a barn-engine, just about the same time that the Old Man got one. A great piece of moderni-sation. It's hard to think of them that way now when those little thumpers are the joy of collectors. One of the clubs had them plonking away in the garden of our local only a week ago last Sunday.

At our place it was the best thing that happened to the boys. Up till then we used to be sent to turn handles on rainy days. One lad each side of the handle we turned the big cast-iron fly wheels – hours with the chaff-cutter, the kibbler, the cake-cracker and the mangold slicer. Now we just listened to the engine and watched the wide, slapping belts. If only the Old Man had managed to mechanise the hay-knife.

Down at the wheelwright's shop Harry got a circular saw, a band-saw and a pillar-drill. And – slicing across history with one blow – he got a lathe. This meant he would never again go down to the water-mill.

From time immemorial – or perhaps just from time medieval – the wheelwright had kept a primitive wooden lathe at the water mill. When the big apple wood naves had to be turned the blocks would be carted down to the mill, an extra belt slipped on the lathe, and the Brandons borrowed a share of the river-power for nave-turning.

The old wooden lathe rotted away unused and so did the saw-pit trestle. And in the village street to the ring of the anvil was added the first throb of industry.

Meanwhile the quietest craftsman of all continued to work next door – the tailor. It's hard to believe that when I was little there was no such thing as reach-me-down clothes in the countryside. But it was so even for poor people. The poorest, of course, dressed in clothes handed on from other people and, in consequence, some of their outfits were quite bizarre. I've seen a hedge-cutter dressed in a swallow-tailed coat and army puttees. An old billy-cock hat was considered to require a bandana handkerchief knotted at the throat and the ends tucked under the braces. The ordinary respectable countryman wore the clothes the tailor made for him. For many years as 'best'; then when they were clearly too old for some special occasion – say the marriage of a daughter to a returning soldier – they were demoted to be working clothes and he returned to the tailor for new ones. But not for a suit. In those earliest days suits were not worn. Certainly the Gentry didn't wear them. In fact we heard that in London they each had both a tailor and a trouser-maker, so that the two halves of their attire were separately chosen and made by different people.

In the circumstances it was better for a man to stick to

the traditional style of broadcloth coat, cord waistcoat and moleskin trousers. These the tailor made for him on average perhaps three times in a lifetime and equipped them with 'bone' buttons that never came off. Actually, they were cowhorn and made by a man who worked in a shed alongside the slaughterhouse.

He also worked in Derby Twist and Cavalry Twill, since the best of his living came from outfitting the estate servants – grooms, gamekeepers, huntsmen – even the parson was allowed a suit a year with his living.

The odds and ends he made into caps for small boys whose clothes were otherwise made at home by Mother. I used to go and watch him sometimes. He sat cross-legged on a low bench – just like the tailor in the book of Grimm's *Fairy Tales* – and I remember he sewed with a very short thread. The economy of that was interesting. He could re-thread a needle so fast – a second and a half I should think – that it was quicker to do that constantly than suffer the inconvenience of sewing with a long thread.

He was a cripple. Many tailors were, and so were saddlers. Village people knew that every boy-child must somehow be given a trade so if a boy was unmistakably crippled they would plan to get him apprenticed to a tailor. So our tailor was a cripple and so, for the same reasons , was the Snob.

There was always a Snob, even in the smallest village. He was the shoemaker and he, similarly, concentrated most of the time on one kind of footware – the hob-nail boot. They were made of the best cow-hide with soles an inch thick and half an inch of welt, handsewn throughout and armoured with rows of hobnails and half-moon irons at toe and heel. We wore them first when we went to school and thenceforward for most of our waking hours.

Women wore them when they went out to help in the fields and little girls even when they had summer pinnies and ribbons in their hair wore them with black woollen stockings for scampering over the countryside. You cannot convince people now how comfortable they were. They ironed out the flints on the roads. They took you through deep puddles without getting wet and they were perfect for making a slide across the playground in wintertime. The weight of them actually helped with walking. They seemed to swing your feet forward and eased you over the miles.

Old boots were old friends. Nobody liked starting on a new pair. But there was a secret to it that in later years we were able to impart to friends in the Army. You put the new boots in a tin bath and then filled it up with hot water. After topping them up hot for a couple of days they were as soft as pulp. Then you put them on wet over new thick socks and went for a ten mile walk. By the time you came back they were the same shape as your feet, and after that they were dried out at a safe distance from the stove and thereafter kept soaked with neatsfoot oil. I have a twenty-three-year-old pair of handsome shooting boots that still bear witness to the virtue of the method.

There was one tiny old man in the village whose craft quite often brought the gentry to his door. He made carriage whips, and they were very beautiful. The forester allowed him to stool certain holly trees up in the woods and thus he grew the holly saplings that at two or three years old were his raw material. He tended them like a gardener. At the time the wild swans were moulting he would wander the river bank collecting their big white quills, the same that in the earlier years were cut into pens. He used them to make a splint joint between holly and whalebone just below where the bow-top of the whip turned over. Every good carriage whip has a swan-quill in it.

Long years before Paddy had come over from Ireland, where his father was a whip-maker, to look for work with horses. We knew that in his prime he had been head nagsman at a distinguished private stable. When he retired he reverted to his father's trade. He also specialised in perfecting the manners of Ladies' hunters and hacks. This was the nearest thing to modern dressage training that we knew in our day and Paddy was the patient master of it.

One evening just as dusk was falling I came upon him sitting on a horse that had stopped at the ford where the stream ran over the road. He was lighting his clay pipe with an air of perfect peace. "What's the matter?" I said, "Won't she go over?" "She'll go over" he said in his squeaky little voice, "even if we're both late for breakfast."

Over the years he squeaked a lot of things to me that taught me about horses. One winter's day I rode Quicksilver out shepherding as a change from Tony, and getting a sniff of the frost in her nostrils she went off bucking all round the Road Field. I just survived it and, as I got her under control, Paddy came through the gate riding one and leading another. "Did you see Paddy?" I cried. "She bucked all round the field but I didn't come off." "Why did you let her buck?" he squeaked.

We never learned the secret of Paddy until after he died. Then the schoolmistress returned in a state of excitement from her weekly reading of *The Times* in the library on Market Day. She had found an obituary notice to Paddy. We all assembled at the school steps for her to read it. Long ago in Zululand as a Corporal of the Household Cavalry he had won the V.C.

And then there were the gypsies, who when I was young

seemed to prefer to be called 'Travellers'. Mr Hughes, the head of one of the local Romany families, used to say "You know Billy Elms, he's a travelling man."

Yet this last year at Appleby Fair a man introduced himself to me and said "I'm a gypsy." I heard the word again several times more and then, listening to other conversations I got an idea why. In the last few years there has been a growing mob of layabouts and ne'er-do-wells who have moved across the land in old lorries and buses. As they camped on farmers' land and seethed across Salisbury Plain they gathered large numbers of police and even more journalists. They call themselves the Travellers, so certainly the word should not be used for Romany people.

The gypsies of our district were well-known and well-liked – as they were in most country districts. We had the Hughes' and the Penfolds' and it was first names all round.

It is a false idea to think of them as people always on their way to the far horizon. In fact, it was the same elsewhere as with us. Each gypsy family had a comparatively small home area – a territory – and they moved within it in a known way. They would be at the right place for the pea-picking and down along the woods when hazel was needed to split for basket-making. Yet, at the boundaries between one territory and another there was contact and information flowed. "We can find you where any travelling man is in the country" they would say. "Just leave it ten days for the word to pass."

Then three or four times a year the Romany people took to the road for the great meeting-places – Epsom Downs, Stow-in-the-Wold, Gallows Hill at Appleby. Here they speak with the voices of their own home district – gypsies with Welsh voices, with a touch of Warwickshire or Yorkshire or the Border. The Essex gypsies have a strong tang of

London. Here they settle their affairs, arrange the marriages. Their daughters build the alliance and their many sons give support and protection. They are the old age pensions and the force of the law. All confrontations must be carried through – rather than lose face – and it may be better for tourists to stay off Gallows Hill as darkness falls.

Their culture is older than ours and many of their customs were brought from far away – like the burning that goes with death.

The old lady of one of our families had become too frail to move around. She parked her van in one place and lived alone there with others coming by to call. All she seemed to ask was a can of milk every day and the can stood clean on the step each morning with a clean washed napkin over it. The lad who brought it from a nearby holding was frightened of her and tried to avoid a sight of her wizened face framed in lace and earrings. But he wondered at the cut-glass windows with the shelves of Crown Derby arranged inside, and the carving and gold-leaf on the Reading Van.

One day when he came down the track it was all gone – nothing left but a pile of warm ashes. It's a tremendous votation to the earth gods and a most unselfish tribute to the dead.

Mrs Penfold used to like to teach me Romany words. What she really liked was to point out how many Romany words we already used. Did I know that Pal is the Romany for brother? And that Koochy which then cropped up in American popular songs is the Romany for pretty? And that Kosh is their word for a stick?

"And what is a sign-post."

I knew that one – "A sign-post is a Pukkering Kosh."

"It is! It is!" she would chuckle. "It's a talking-stick that tells you where you're going! And a Pukkerer is a talker, like Mrs Kent!" Mrs Kent was certainly the top Pukkerer in our village. She would spend two hours of the morning on the door-step with anyone who would let her.

There was a woman who was a relative of the Penfolds who came through now and again to visit them. She drove a painted gypsy pot-cart and wore very fine clothes. She was a Dukkerer, a fortune-teller, or literally, "a weaver of spells." She used to call on Mrs Kent and showed infinite patience in indulging her failing. In the following days she would knock on the doors of the district and offer her magic readings. She said to one young wife "I have a beautiful surprise for you. You're going to have a baby at last." The girl was greatly excited. "Are you sure?" she said, "The doctor said Monday that he couldn't say for certain!" So, you see, every Dukkerer needs a Pukkerer.

Of course, the people of property didn't like them and urged their strappers against them. The police were against them, having at that time the primary purpose of protecting property and resenting the fact that the Romany kept their troubles to themselves. "We got on well with the Dear Sirs" said a woman in the Forest to me. They called the gypsies by that name on account of the mode of address they used. "We were all friends. Then after the war the well-to-do came and bought houses and got on the council. They wouldn't have them. Sent the keepers at night to tip them out of their beds."

One sort of gypsies very well understood the well-to-do. That is the horse-dealers. The biggest of them that we knew was Ted Wing. Biggest, that is, in his operations. In person he was a tiny little man with his cap on straight and his gaiters polished and his whip held in a beautiful pair of dogskin gloves like the coach-men used to use.

He turned up one Saturday morning just after the hunters were coming up from grass at the yard of a house belonging to a millionaire brewer – a name now known on many bottles. It was his custom at a weekend to inspect his string and try them out, giving his authoritative orders to a file of cap-touching stable staff.

Ted rode into the yard on a fine chestnut and showed he could touch his cap with the best.

"What's that you've got there, Wing?"

"It's the horse for you if ever I saw it."

"Oh, indeed – how much money?"

"I wouldn't come to money, Sir, not till I was sure of it. Anyone else and I'd say it was sound. But I wouldn't try to fool you, Sir. A while ago I thought I might have heard just a whisper in it's wind."

The brewer had it galloped on and listened to the wind. He put it in the stable and gave its wind time to settle and listened again.

"That horse is sound in wind, Wing."

"I'd want nobody else's word for it, Sir. The price is four hundred pounds." A lot of money then.

The horse was led for a week and then the new owner decided to try it over jumps. It knocked a gate off its latches and galloped straight through an oxer fence.

Blind in one eye and nearly blind in the other. So never let a conjurer catch your attention with his other hand.

Ted Wing is gone now, and so are nearly all the old men who limped about the village. A back that never recovered from loading corn. A thumb that was lost in the woods. A neck that acquired a poking thrust from being put into turnip fields with a hoe and left there for ten days. A hip that broke when a cow tipped a man over a gate as he walked between her and a hidden calf.

As you played dominoes in the snug you could tell when the ploughman was coming. Plink – Plonk. Plink – Plonk. After years of one foot on the land and the other in the furrow he couldn't walk any other way.

They never knew the difference between work and leisure. They lived by the now disgraced work ethic and derived their manhood from it.

The corn was put in canvas West of England sacks and each weighed two and a quarter hundredweight. "Just lift that one up in the Waggon, Sonny." A grown man could do it if his muscles were hardened and if he had the timing. It was – hup on the feet – hup on the knees – hup on the shoulder – hup up on the tailboard! We used to start trying it at fourteen.

At the village fete they tossed double-size corn sheafs up over a sort of rugger goal-post set at the full height of a load. The pitching-fork handle was fourteen feet long and, when the weight had reached forty-five degrees you could follow the strain down the bending handle and the same curve of the man's spine.

Never again, I think, will men do so much work, with such great skill for so little money and such an absence of self-pity.

A black man once rang a bell for me in America. He rang such a big bell that I thought about him for days.

He was a soldier. In fact, he was the first black man ever to rise to the rank of General of the Army which is the American equivalent of Field Marshal.

This was great news and the Pentagon had arranged a Media Presentation which was packed with journalists.

They had done their homework. They had discovered that he was born in a shack in a little Southern share-cropping settlement and perhaps didn't wear shoes until he joined the army.

This is what they wanted to know about. He wanted to talk about soldiering but it was borne in on him that in the end he would have to address this question.

"Tell us, Sir" said the next reporter, "When you were young you must have been very poor indeed?"

The General gave him a polite smile "I guess you're right," he said. "But I'm going to tell you something. We were so da-a-a-a-mn busy enjoying ourselves that we never noticed."

Great honour and good luck to him. I like to think that in the place he came from they might have had china christening mugs for little boy-children that bore the same inscriptions as they used to in our district –

Swift is the Hare
   And Wise is the Fox

This little Calf
   Will grow into an Ox

He' get his living
   Among the thorns

And die like his Dad
   With a great pair of horns

1889 – 1929

This has been about country life from the time Mother first met the Old Man until I left the farm to go to London University and read Veterinary Science.

After that the world changed.